From Buttons to Conversations

A Revolution in User Experience

Chad Michel

Apress®

From Buttons to Conversations: A Revolution in User Experience

Chad Michel
LINCOLN, NE, USA

ISBN-13 (pbk): 979-8-8688-2687-0   ISBN-13 (electronic): 979-8-8688-2688-7
https://doi.org/10.1007/979-8-8688-2688-7

Managing Director, Apress Media LLC: Welmoed Spahr
Acquisitions Editor: Ryan Byrnes
Development Editor: Laura Berendson
Editorial Assistant: Gryffin Winkler

Cover designed by eStudioCalamar

Distributed to the book trade worldwide by Springer Science+Business Media New York, 1 New York Plaza, New York, NY 10004. Phone 1-800-SPRINGER, fax (201) 348-4505, e-mail orders-ny@springer-sbm.com, or visit www.springeronline.com. Apress Media, LLC is a Delaware LLC and the sole member (owner) is Springer Science + Business Media Finance Inc (SSBM Finance Inc). SSBM Finance Inc is a **Delaware** corporation.

For information on translations, please e-mail booktranslations@springernature.com; for reprint, paperback, or audio rights, please e-mail bookpermissions@springernature.com.

Apress titles may be purchased in bulk for academic, corporate, or promotional use. eBook versions and licenses are also available for most titles. For more information, reference our Print and eBook Bulk Sales web page at http://www.apress.com/bulk-sales.

Any source code or other supplementary material referenced by the author in this book is available to readers on GitHub. For more detailed information, please visit https://www.apress.com/gp/services/source-code.

If disposing of this product, please recycle the paper

*To my beloved wife Lisa, my son Sam, and my daughter Eva.
You are my home, my heart, and my greatest story. Thank you for every laugh, every quiet moment, and every reason I keep writing. And to my dog Ellie, for keeping my feet warm.*

Table of Contents

About the Author

 **Chad Michel** is CTO for Don't Panic Labs with more than 20 years of software development and engineering experience. He holds a bachelor's degree in computer engineering and a master's degree in computer science. At Don't Panic Labs, he works with clients to solve problems through innovative software solutions. Chad has worked for several companies in Lincoln, helping build a practice management application for lawyers, developing key features for an ecommerce application, and wrangling an Internet content delivery system into a stable platform. He regularly speaks at technical meetups hosted by Don't Panic Labs with significant contributions to the company blog. He also enjoys contributing at technical conferences and groups. Chad teaches Cloud Architecture and Applied AI at the University of Nebraska-Lincoln. Chad enjoys combat sports and frequently trains taekwondo and Brazilian Jiu-Jitsu.

About the Technical Reviewer

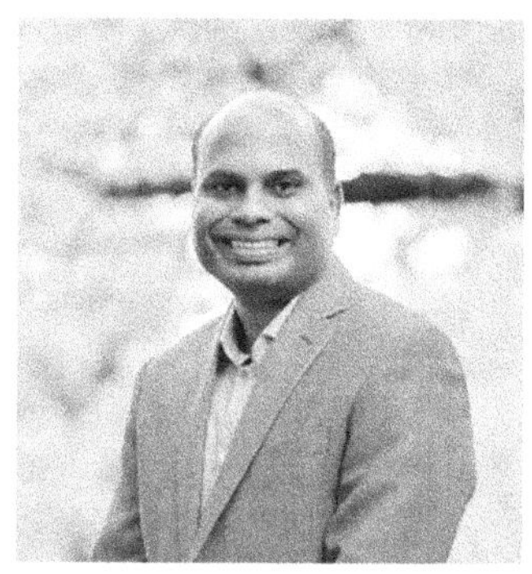 **Likhesh Bramhanwade** is a Software Development Manager at Amazon, leading teams that build large-scale platforms for invoicing, B2B compliance, personalization, and AI-driven customer experiences. He has more than 21 years of experience across Amazon, Nordstrom, and NTT DATA, specializing in cloud-native architectures, low-latency services, advertising systems, and B2B integrations. He is a Certified Scrum Master (CSM) and Certified Scrum Product Owner (CSPO) with more than a decade of hands-on experience applying Agile practices. Likhesh is a Fellow of IETE, a Senior Member of IEEE, and an active technical community contributor as a reviewer, speaker, and mentor. He is passionate about applying generative AI and agentic workflows to shape the next generation of digital commerce, payments, and B2B integrations.

Acknowledgments

This book is the continued exploration of how to create better software. None of this would have happened without the great team at Don't Panic Labs and the great partners I have worked with over the last few years. Don't Panic Labs serves as a great opportunity to refine processes and skills because of the number of projects and the diversity of projects we have been lucky to work on.

A special shout-out to Doug Durham for keeping us focused on engineering excellence, building great software, and nurturing a learning-first culture.

Introduction

I started writing software in the 1990s. Back then, software development and user experience felt like a very specific, very rigid machine. Users pressed buttons, filled out forms, and navigated menus. We, as software creators, designed those buttons, forms, and menus. It was a predictable relationship, and honestly, a comfortable one.

Then something started to shift.

The shift wasn't sudden. It happened quietly, in increments, like the water rising before a flood. First, users started expecting more. Then JavaScript grew up and gave us the ability to build richer experiences in the browser. I feel user experience stalled for a while, with each development team trying to create better web experiences, but they were all creating derivatives of each other. And now, and this is the part that matters for this book, we have AI.

Not AI as a buzzword, not AI as a feature you bolt onto an existing product to write "AI-powered" in the marketing copy, I mean, AI that can help users complete their tasks. That kind of AI changes everything about your user experience.

The book is about that change.

If you've spent time in product design, UX, or software development, you already know that building great user experiences is hard. Everyone who uses software has opinions about software, which means your users are always critics. You've constantly been balancing usability, accessibility, and the context while someone is asking why the button isn't a slightly different shade of blue. It's a tough job.

What I've come to believe is that AI gives us a real shot at making that job easier, and more importantly, at making software genuinely better for the people who use it. Conversational interfaces aren't just a trend. They're the most natural way humans communicate, and for the first time in the history of software, we have the technology to make them actually work.

I wrote this book because I wanted to give you a clear-eyed look at what's changing, what it means in practice, and how to move forward without panicking. We'll start with the foundations, why user experience matters, and how we got to where we are. From there, we'll walk through the shift to conversational experiences, the technologies that make them possible, and how to integrate them into real systems.

By the end of this book, my goal is simple. I want you to be the person in the room who can say confidently, "Here's how we should approach this." Not because you memorized a framework, but because you understand the principles well enough to apply them to whatever situation you're in.

The wave is coming. Let's make sure you're ready to ride it.

CHAPTER 1

The Human–Computer Interface

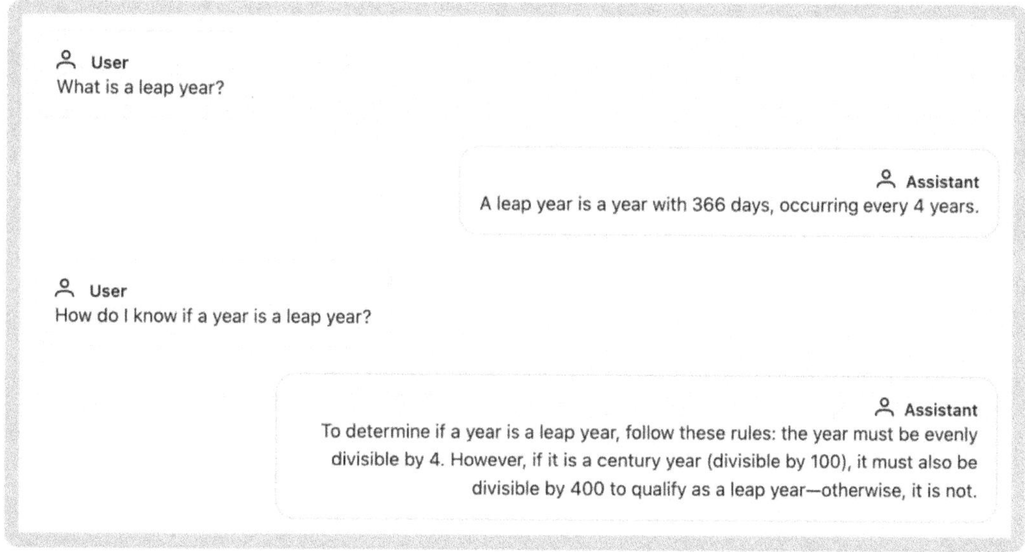

Figure 1-1. *AI conversation about leap years, and how to calculate if a year is a leap year*

This chapter traces the evolution of how humans interact with computers, from punch cards and command lines to graphical interfaces, and now, AI-driven conversational systems. We explore the shift in interface design that changed who could use software and how effectively they could use it, and why understanding this history matters as we design the next generation of user experiences.

Leap years happen basically every four years (Figure 1-1). And when we have a leap year, we gain 1 extra day, which is February 29. The rules of which year is a leap year are more complicated than you would imagine. Typically, we think leap years are every 4

C. Michel, *From Buttons to Conversations*, https://doi.org/10.1007/979-8-8688-2688-7_1

years, but if the year is divisible by 100, that year usually isn't a leap year. But 2000 was a leap year, why? Because it was divisible by 400. At the time of this writing, the year is 2026. So, when will be the next leap year?

Obviously 2028. Wrong, I think 2026 is a leap year. Because of the massive change in how we interact with software, I believe 2026 will be a year we make a major change in technology. The rate of technical changes has skyrocketed over the last few years. And what we can do with software is exploding, effectively making each year a leap year, or at least we are making a leap in technology.

Software is written for humans. Software is written to aid a business process. Software is written to allow for the creation of products. But in all cases, there is some form of user experience and some interface between the user and the software.

There have been a variety of interfaces between computers and people over the years. The early days of computers were fairly manual. Humans created punch cards and used manual switches to interact with computers. Computers communicated back to the user using lights and switches.

In the 1960s, computers upgraded to command-line interfaces (CLIs) (Figure 1-2). Humans could type commands, and computers would execute them. In some ways, much of my favorite software still runs this way. I use git for source control (as does almost everyone else), and git still is a series of commands we execute from a terminal.

```
FromButtonsToConversationsClassMaterials % git status
On branch main
Your branch is up to date with 'origin/main'.

Changes not staged for commit:
  (use "git add <file>..." to update what will be committed)
  (use "git restore <file>..." to discard changes in working directory)
        modified:   1-Welcome/slides.md
        modified:   7-Appendex-Sample Data/slides.md

no changes added to commit (use "git add" and/or "git commit -a")
```

Figure 1-2. *Command-line interface example*

In 1968, the world changed when Douglas Engelbart delivered the "Mother of All Demos." In this demo, he showed how a display, keyboard, and a mouse could be used to interface with a computer. This didn't spawn an immediate move into GUIs (Graphic User Interface), partially because hardware was not ready.

In the 1970s and even into the early 1980s, the command line continued to rule. But Apple, with its launch of the Macintosh computer line, changed the world forever. And we entered the era of GUIs.

GUIs solved a non-obvious problem. Many people think they just made software better. But better is difficult to define. One way GUIs are better is that they are easier to use and learn. The software can guide you to your goal. There have been a variety of studies showing that GUIs do have many benefits. A study involving nurses showed that nurses using GUIs committed fewer errors, had faster learning, and higher user satisfaction.

But easier to use, is often defined as what is easier for non-experts. I am calling this out in particular because an expert in software will often be faster with CLIs (Command-Line Interfaces, where all interaction is done by typing text commands into a terminal rather than clicking buttons or menus) or more crude interfaces. GUIs are often not better for advanced users.

The rise of Generative AI (GenAI) is bringing significant change in how we think about software interfaces. These AI systems, built on large language models (LLMs), can understand and generate text. For the first time, the interface can adapt to the user rather than requiring the user to adapt to the interface.

GenAI tools are now being integrated into developer workflows, bringing conversational AI interfaces to command-line and coding environments. These tools represent a new layer of integration between developers and systems.

As I write this chapter, one of the most popular tools for developers I know is Claude Code. Claude Code is an unapologetically CLI tool. It is an AI development assistant that doubles down on the CLI interface. Claude Code probably isn't going to be as good for new or learning developers. But for developers who want to get things done, it is probably a great tool.

And back to my example of git. Because I learned git when there wasn't much for GUIs I learned at a pretty deep level, and have continued to use the CLI as my primary interface to git. But newer developers often learn git as part of some GUI, and usually don't have a need to learn the CLI at this point. I can probably be a little faster with the CLI than they can be with a GUI, but that little performance gain is probably not enough for them to switch (Figure 1-3).

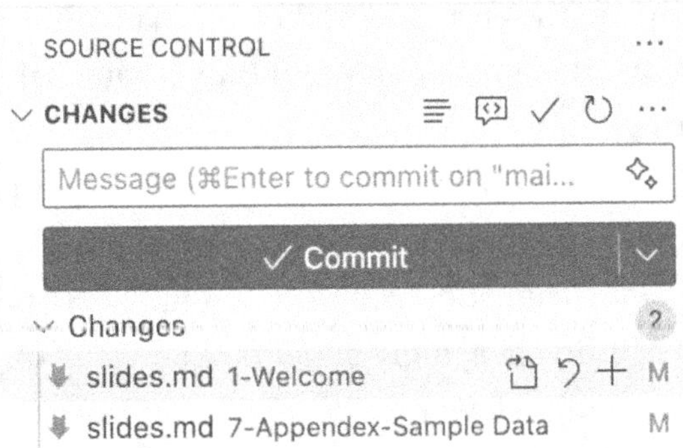

Figure 1-3. *Git GUI interface*

And my usage of git is also an interesting study in the advantage of GUIs over CLIs in visualization. When it comes to doing source code comparisons, I now find myself using the GUIs of VS Code or GitHub to do those comparisons.

Figures 1-4 and 1-5 show the command line comparison vs. the visual.

```
---
theme: apple-basic
info: |
-   ## Technology Innovations
-   AI and technologies enabling conversational UI
+   ## From Buttons to Conversations
+   Appende - Sample Data
drawings:
    persist: false
```

Figure 1-4. *Command line diff comparison*

```
1  ---                                                              1  ---
2  theme: apple-basic                                              2  theme: apple-basic
3  info: |                                                         3  info: |
4-   ## Technology Innovations                              →      4+   ## From Buttons to Conversations
5-   AI and technologies enabling conversational UI         +      5+   Appende - Sample Data
6  drawings:                                                       6  drawings:
7    persist: false                                                7    persist: false
8  transition: slide-left                                          8  transition: slide-left
9  title: From Buttons to Conversations - Technology Innovations   9  title: From Buttons to Conversations - Technology Innovations
10 mdc: true                                                       10 mdc: true
11 ---                                                             11 ---
```

Figure 1-5. *Visual diff comparison in VS Code*

In the above pictures, in both cases, I can compare the changes to some slides in a slides.md file. But with a visual interface, I can be given extra tools. These include tools to accept or discard each change individually. Also, with a visual GUI, it is easier to layer in additional visuals, such as spellcheck indicators. Notice the misspelled word?

GUIs are also often better at showing relationships. You can come up with some crazy ASCII art to demonstrate the relationships (Figure 1-6), but GUIs enable more abilities.

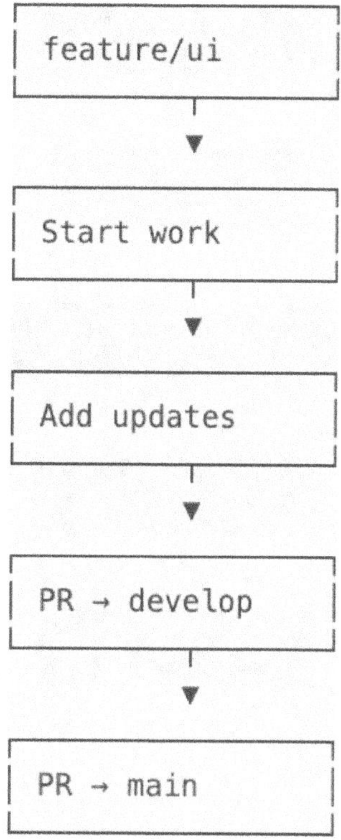

Figure 1-6. *ASCII art diagram*

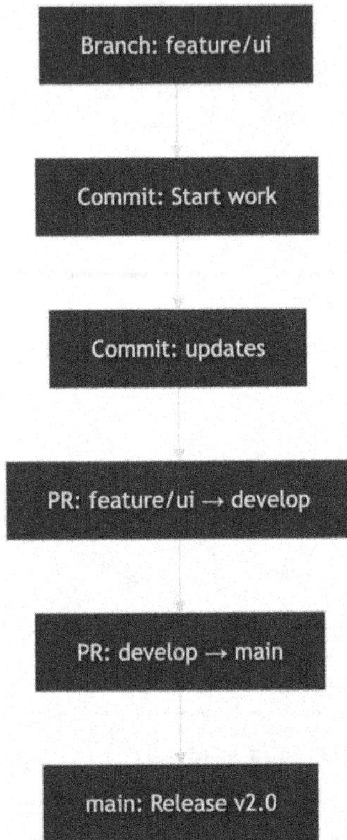

Figure 1-7. *GUI diagram*

This trend toward richer user interfaces (Figure 1-7) has enabled more people to use software and required less training. Our ability to build better user interfaces has enabled us to enable more users to use software.

Definition of User Experience

As we explore how AI will change the future of user experience, we might want to define user experience. Since we are asking how AI will change user experience, maybe we should ask AI to define User Experience (Figure 1-8).

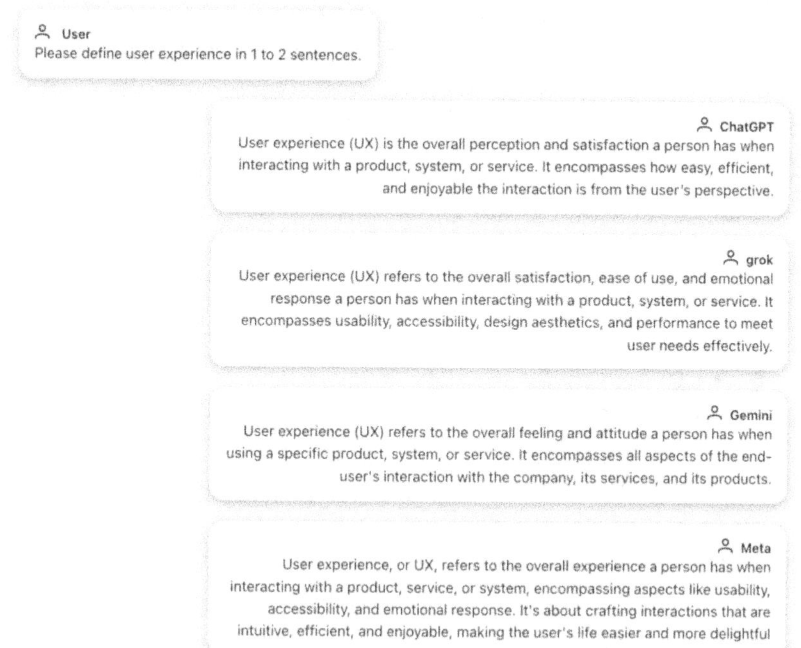

Figure 1-8. *AI definitions of user experience*

Each definition provided a similar response. The responses are not the same, but we can draw some common conclusions.

- Satisfaction/Delight

- Usability

- Accessibility

User experience could be defined as "A software system's ability to enable all users to enjoy completing tasks." Now that definition might be a little more biased toward enjoyment than much business software is geared toward. For most business software, we might want the definition to use "quickly" instead of "enjoy."

A good example of why quickly is often more important than enjoyment would be the classic green screen software systems. These are terminals that are connected to a mainframe. The software written for these green screens looks archaic (and is archaic). But watch a master of that software work, and you can be in the presence of a virtuoso, navigating, updating, searching at an almost mind-blowing pace. Sure, the software is hard to train. Sure, the software runs on old hardware (Figure 1-9), but the people who master those old green screen systems are extremely effective.

```
=== CRM TERMINAL v2.1 ===
Customer Relationship Management System

FIRST_NAME      : John
LAST_NAME       : Smith

EMAIL           : john.smith@company.com
PHONE           : +1-555-0123
COMPANY         : Tech Solutions Inc
POSITION        : CTO
DEAL_VALUE      : $45,000
STATUS          : QUALIFIED_LEAD
```

Figure 1-9. *Classic green screen terminal*

Replacing green screens with a web interface can be a very hard sell to those users. New users who don't understand the system will easily buy into a web interface. But the existing master user of a system will often complain about the transition. And a key reason, they used to be faster. As we build systems, we cannot just ignore these complaints. We must build faster systems. Users should be more efficient with our new systems, not worse.

But, as we move into this new age of user experience, we must not assume the current status is acceptable. Products that lean heavily into this new world will leap past us. We must leap forward.

Why Does UX Matter?

UX is how our users interact with our software, and by extension, how users judge our software. If our user experience is bad, users will assume our software is bad.

And UX is an interesting field in software development. In most areas, the vast majority of people don't really know much about the concepts. Many people understand databases as a concept, but most don't know how to design tables. And most users know they don't know how to design tables.

That is not true for user experience. For user experience, everyone is an expert. That statement will seem like hyperbole to many, but I mean it. Everyone uses software all the time. Everyone knows what they like and dislike. To a degree, everyone is an expert.

We must approach UX with an awareness that everyone has opinions and everyone believes their opinions are right. With UX we need to find ways to define better/worse in a way that can be debated, or we should assume it is only a matter of opinion and move on from the debate.

Approach of This Book

This book hopes to provide exposure and some thought-provoking concepts for anyone inside of user experience, product design, or software construction. This should provide you with more confidence to be the person who says, "We should do X," with that product meeting discussion.

Building confidence involves a few things. This book will provide both knowledge and the follow-along experience of building a CRM's user experience using some of these new tools. CRMs are Contact Relationship Management systems. They excel at tracking the contacts and leads in a sales process.

In Chapter 2, we will build a base of classic understanding of user experience design. This classic understanding will focus on user experience as used for web development. Here, we will define terms as they will be used in this book, and define many common user experience patterns. In Chapter 2, we will show how many pieces of the UX would be built in a classic forms world.

In Chapter 3, we will discuss the changes enabled by these new AI tools. Here, we will dive into the revolution of changing our user experience from forms into conversations. We will walk through how we could reimage our CRM system, thinking conversation first.

Chapter 4 focuses on the technology and the new features it enables. Here, we will dive deeper into the new technologies and how we can use them to create conversational experiences. Here, we will look into how we will apply these technologies to build a modern CRM system.

In Chapter 5, we will look at how to integrate these new experiences into legacy applications. There is more legacy software than new software going to be worked on, and we must have approaches to integrate and extend our existing systems with these new features.

Finally, Chapter 6 will bring together these concepts and a look forward to how these conversational systems will continue to evolve. Chapter 6 provides a view into the future of our user experiences.

Summary

This chapter retells the history of the human–computer interface. From the cruder interfaces of the early computing era, through the command-line interface, and then through the graphical user interfaces. Today we are entering a new revolution, the revolution to GenAI and agentic systems.

Key Takeaways

- Interface design directly impacts who can use software and how effectively they can learn int.

- Better interfaces for beginners do not always work better for experts.

- Generative AI introduces a new approach where the interfaces can adapt to users rather than requiring users to learn or adapt to the interface.

Bibliography

Staggers, N., and Kobus, D. (2000). Comparing response time, errors, and satisfaction between text-based and graphical user interfaces during nursing order tasks. *Journal of the American Medical Informatics Association, 7*(2), 164–176. `https://doi.org/10.1136/jamia.2000.0070164`

CHAPTER 2

Forms, Controls, and Buttons

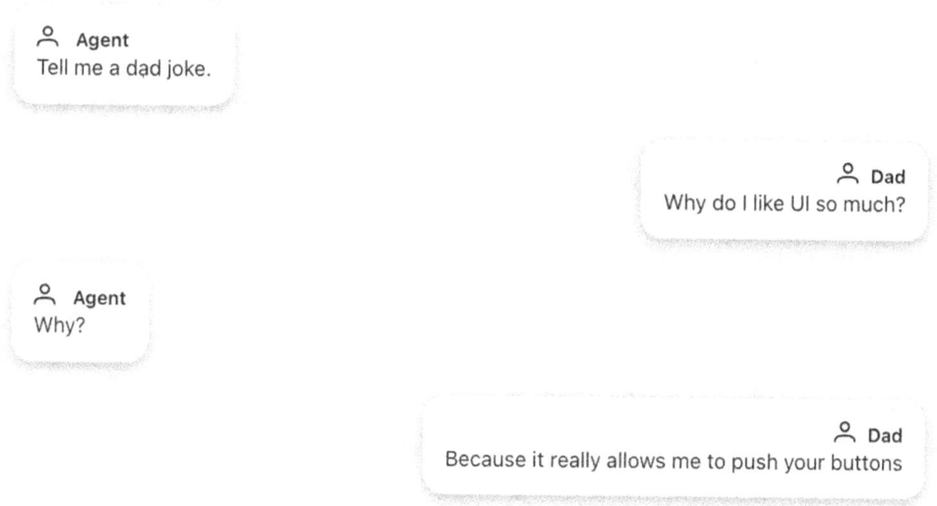

Figure 2-1. *Forms, controls, and buttons in modern user interfaces*

User experience is more complicated than it seems, a large part of that complication is because we must balance many competing desires within systems. And when we factor in different user types, this problem is even more complex. Figure 2-1 gives a glimpse of a chat user experience, which contains text, layout, and a dad joke.

This chapter provides a background on user experience and user experience design. Many topics are covered here, many of which could be entire books themselves. This does mean we are doing a sort of tour-da-design. We are covering a lot of material, but having a rough understanding of these concepts and how I am using them will be helpful in understanding later chapters in this book.

© Chad Michel 2026
C. Michel, *From Buttons to Conversations*, https://doi.org/10.1007/979-8-8688-2688-7_2

We have tended to create more complex user experiences. When creating websites in the early 2000s, we were largely living inside of the standard HTML box for things we could do. Today, almost every application is using a variety of complex controls and tools. In the early 2000s, if an application had chat as part of it, the application was a chat application. Today, something as complex as chat is just a feature for an existing application.

Users are demanding more. And if we don't give users better user experiences, they will find them elsewhere. Others will provide a better user experience, and ultimately take our customers.

A primary goal of this chapter is to ensure we have a solid base of understanding and common ground before we take on abstract concepts. In part, this chapter will attempt to define many of the common terms used in user experience. This will be the jumping off point for our next chapters where we discuss the evolution of these existing patterns.

Computers exist to solve problems for people. Usually, this involves automating or simplifying an existing real-world task for users. If we continue the CRM mentioned in Chapter 1, we can use that example as a discussion point for how optimize the experience of a user of a CRM system.

CRM stands for Contact Relationship Management. Most companies use some sort of CRM system to aid in their sales processes. CRM systems exist for the management of contacts (obviously), leads, opportunities, activities, quotes, and invoices. Often, CRMs will manage things like support tickets/cases, campaigns.

Since CRMs are heavily focused on managing business processes, they will have many dashboards optimized for showing the status of those processes. A value of CRMs is this process management and oversight. These systems are extremely common and have existed for a long time.

CRM systems have existed since the age of green screens, terminal-based applications. Figure 2-2 shows what one of these early systems looked like. Terminal applications have a limited number of controls and features that can be used to enhance the user experience, but don't let that make you think their user experience is bad. Many terminal applications have incredibly speedy user interfaces for users who understand how to use them. Often, users don't want to leave terminal applications, because anything that replaces them will make the use slower, especially until they learn the new system. Users of terminal applications almost always forget how much effort it was to learn the terminal application in the first place.

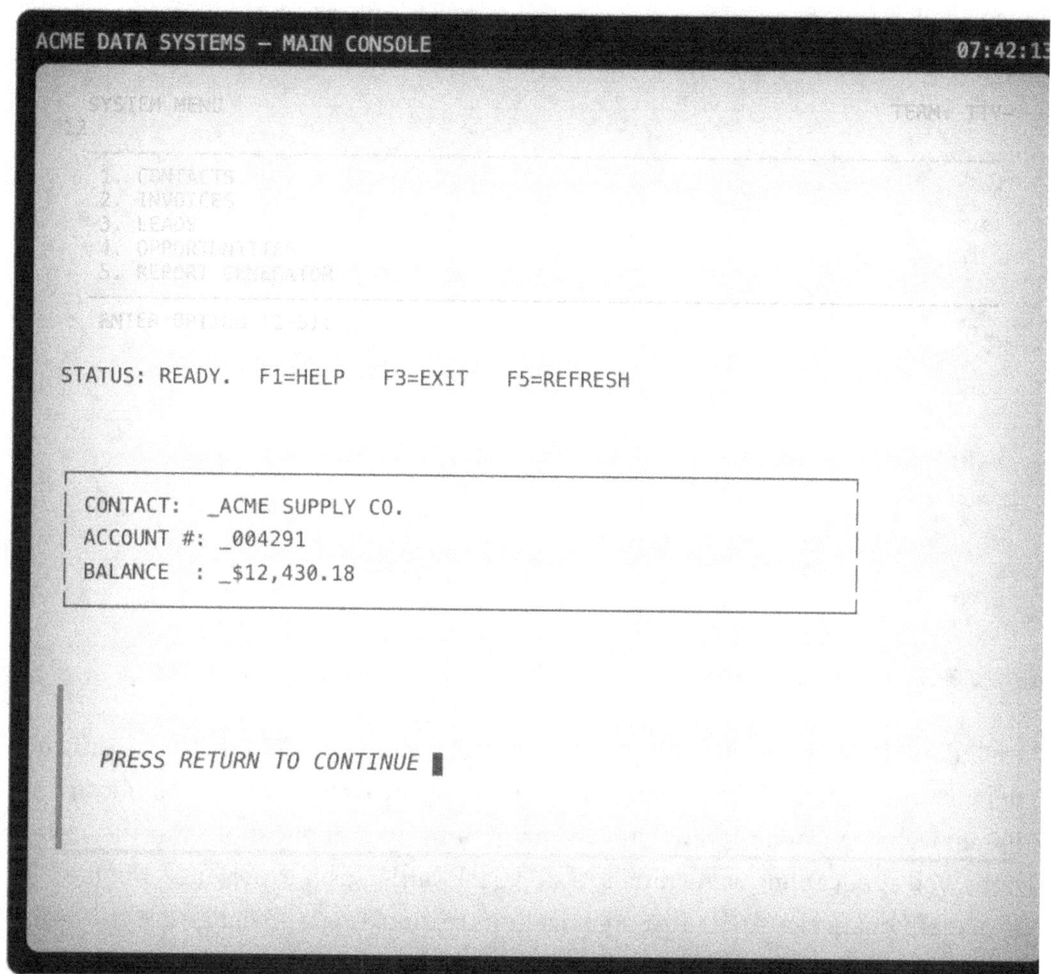

Figure 2-2. *Terminal-based CRM application*

I came up writing software during the 1990s, which means I wrote some Windows Forms–style applications. I think these are best known for their consistent gray (or battleship gray) look. These applications were usually pretty speedy and required direct access to local network resources to work. Deployment of these was often custom, which made deployments problematic and risky. Figure 2-3 shows a Customer Manager screen in a windows form style.

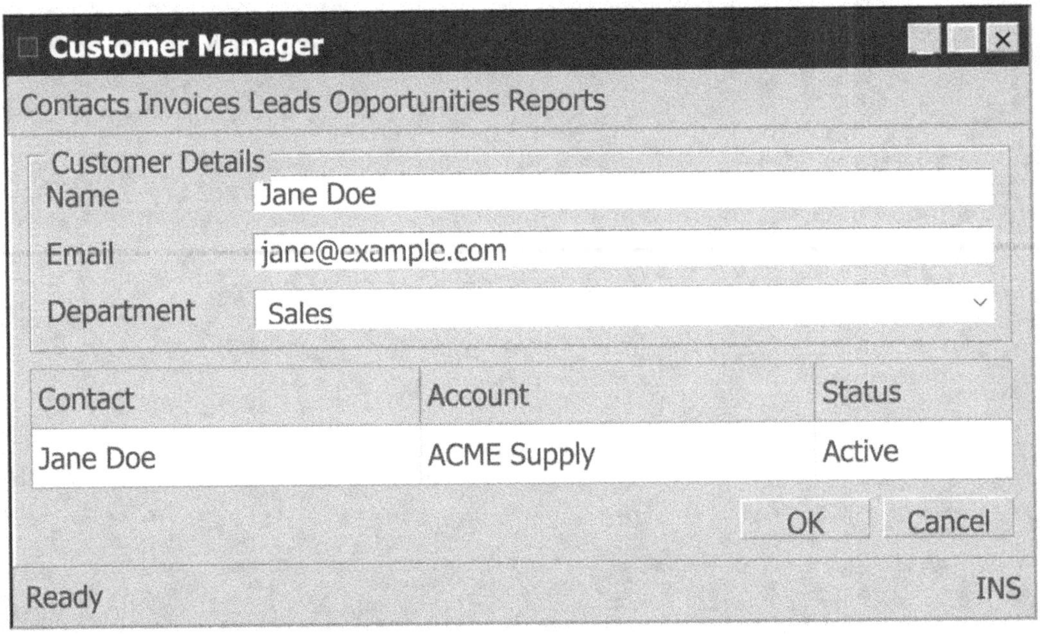

Figure 2-3. *Windows Forms–style application with rich user interface*

Windows Form applications had very rich user experiences, but they were difficult to deploy, which made them difficult to maintain. As the web took off, the ability to maintain web applications grew. Quickly maintaining web applications was the easiest option. Web applications were initially a step backward in user experience, but the ease of maintenance pushed most organizations to quickly adopt. Figure 2-4 shows an example of an early web application experience.

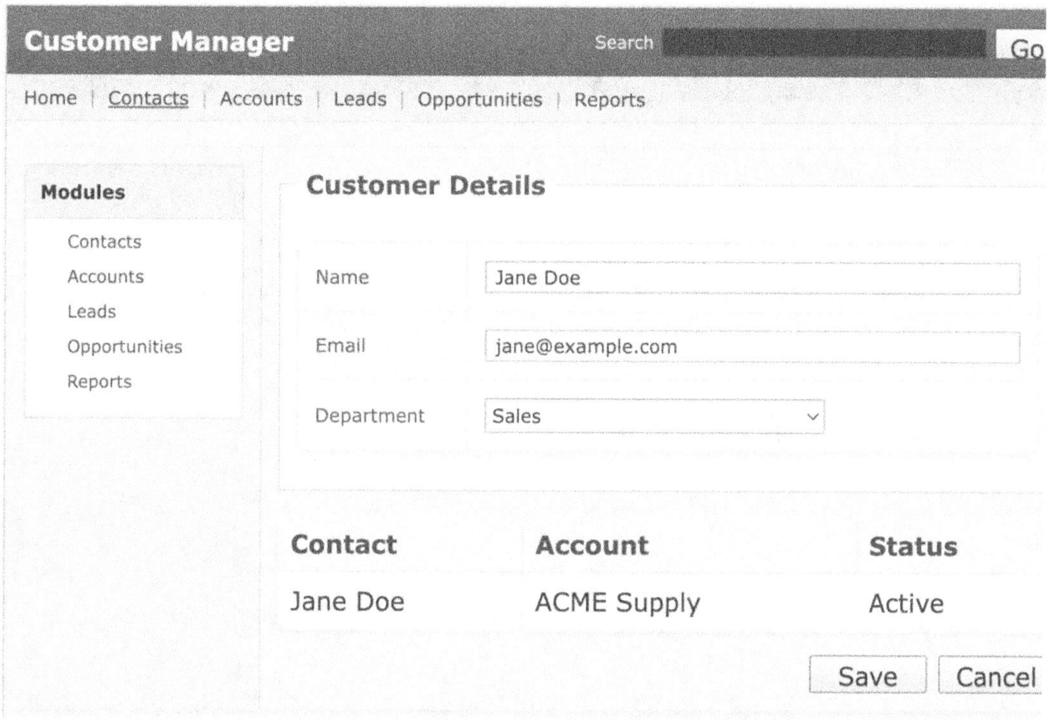

Figure 2-4. *Early web application with limited interactivity*

Web application had many limitations, but surprisingly, web applications had a secret hero, JavaScript. JavaScript, a language many of us loathed for years (including me), quickly proved itself to be a great language for building user experiences.

JavaScript and the many frameworks written to create better user interfaces allowed us to build user interfaces richer than the Windows Forms we had before, but with the deployment model of web applications. This gave us the best of both worlds.

Now, many people will scoff at modern web applications being as rich as Windows Forms (or other native technologies), but from a practical building of business application we are there. Figure 2-5 shows a modern contact form built on web technologies.

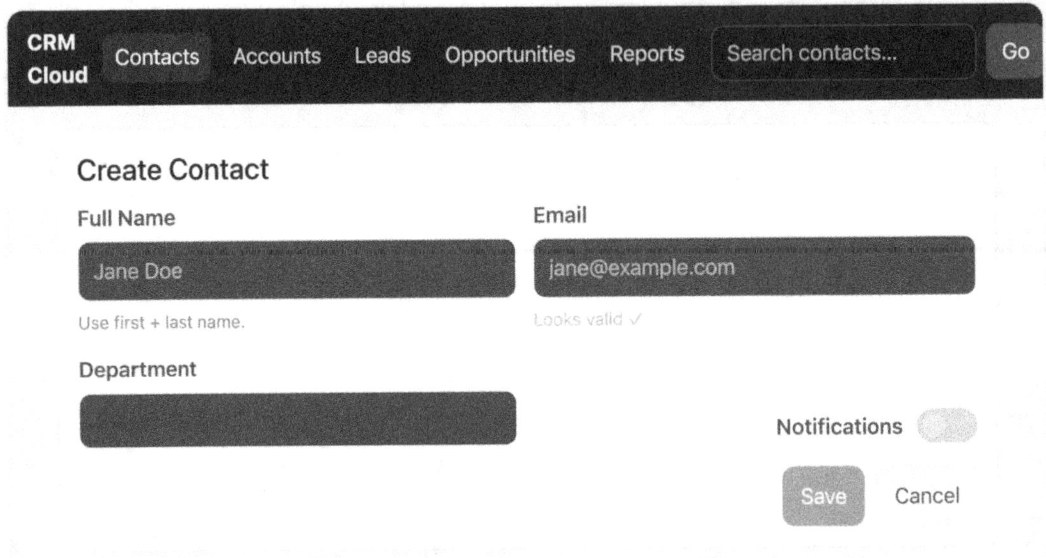

Figure 2-5. *Modern web application with JavaScript-powered user experience*

I am not saying that these modern web applications are without problems. The fact that a second language that lives on top of JavaScript, TypeScript, might be a sign that the base is a little shaky. But what has been achieved is amazing. When you imagine that Microsoft Excel runs in JavaScript in the browser, that is impressive.

All of these features available to us haven't necessarily made the application better. The art of combining these new features has created a role within organizations called a user experience designer, also known as a product designer. Product designers, or user experience designers, must balance many factors when creating great user experiences.

Aspects of User Experience

Good user experience balances many aspects. Some of these are more obvious, but all of these are important. We are covering these here because they are ways to evaluate the quality of the user experiences we create.

1. Usability

2. Accessibility

3. Affordance

4. Context

5. Hierarchy

6. Consistency

7. Progressive Disclosure

8. Error Handling & Recovery

Usability

Usability is obviously a big part of our goals with any user experience. We want to create experiences that are easy to learn, use, and accomplish tasks efficiently. Great user interfaces should require no documentation for the user, it should be obvious.

Figure 2-6 is an example of a bad contact edit form. There are no labels, appears to have no validation, and the button actions are not clear.

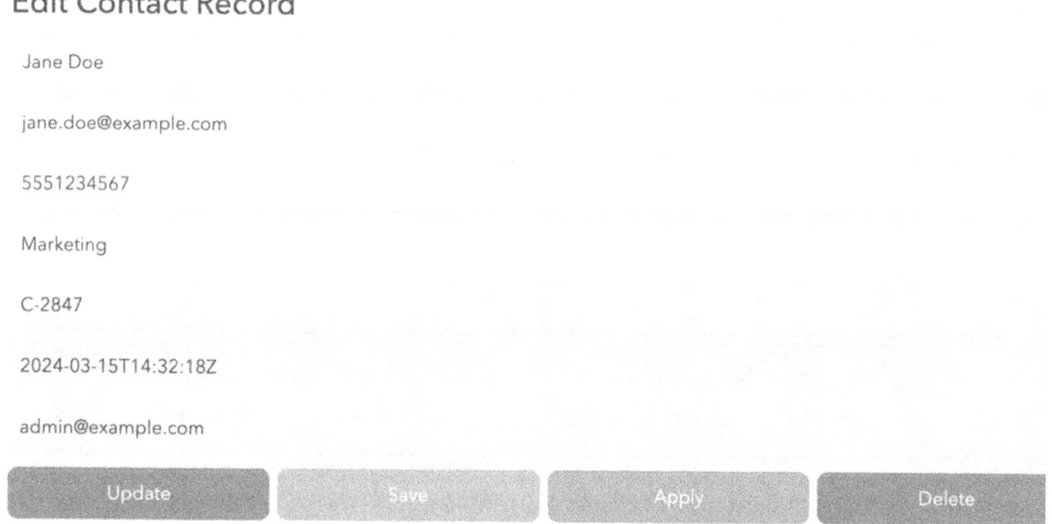

Figure 2-6. *Poor usability example: Contact form lacking labels and validation*

Figure 2-7 is a cleaned-up version, with clear labels, email validation, clear primary and secondary actions.

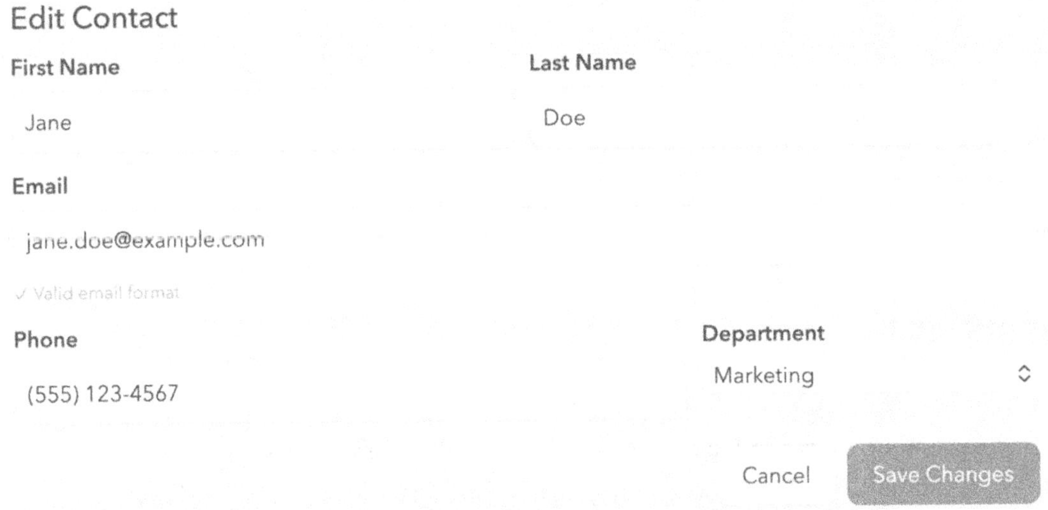

Figure 2-7. Improved usability: Contact form with clear labels and validation

Accessibility

Accessibility means creating interfaces that work for all users, including those with disabilities. Sometimes accessibility is shortened to a11y (a then 11 characters, then y). This is an interesting aspect of user experience design, because it is not just good to do, but it is the law. For more information about the legal requirements, I recommend looking at WCAG (Web Content Accessibility Guidelines).

When it comes to building websites, I always go back to the WCAG principles, they are the foundation for building great software. The four big ones spell out POUR. Content has to be Perceivable so people can actually see or hear it no matter how they access the page. Operable so anyone can navigate and interact with it whether they're using a mouse, keyboard, or assistive tech. Understandable so the language and layout make sense without confusing anyone. Robust so it works reliably across different browsers devices, and future tools. If you are not hitting these POUR (Perceivable, Operable, Understandable, Robust) principles we are probably building bad software.

Also, we are very lucky in that there are many tools that can help us achieve this goal. Accessibility (a11y) tools:

- Axe-Core is an open source accessibility testing engine. Great for developer that want to automate the testing for accessibility.

- Lighthouse (in Google's Chrome Browser) is a tool that already exists inside of Chrome and can be used to evaluate your application against accessibility standards.

Figure 2-8 is a user experience example showing many user experience accessibility issues. Notice the low contrast with the colors. The unclear focus behavior. And clear labels.

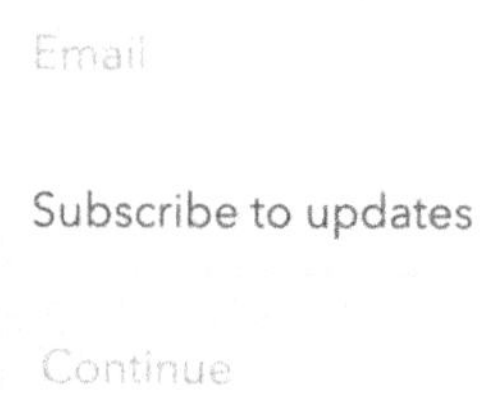

Email

Subscribe to updates

Continue

Figure 2-8. *Accessibility issues: Low contrast and poor labeling*

Figure 2-9 shows a better version from an accessibility perspective. The contrast is better. The labeling is much improved, and we can clearly see the focusable controls.

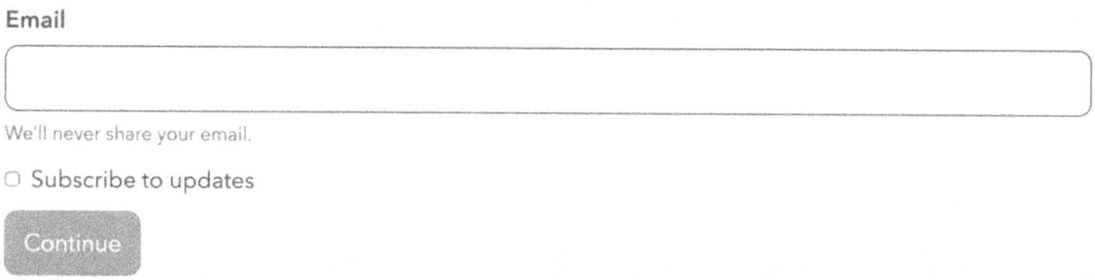

Email

We'll never share your email.

○ Subscribe to updates

Continue

Figure 2-9. *Better accessibility: Improved contrast and clear labeling*

Many accessibility problems fall into a few categories:

- Visual (low contrast, missing alt tags)

- Keyboard (usable without a mouse)

- Auditory (missing captions/transcripts)

- Cognitive (unclear language)

- Inaccessible forms/navigation (missing labels, confusing links)

Affordance

Visual cues that suggest how an element should be used. Buttons should appear clickable; use radio vs. checkboxes correctly; the system should provide correct feedback.

In the example below (Figure 2-10), the buttons are not clearly buttons, the file upload area is not obvious, and there is no clear visual hierarchy.

Figure 2-10. *Poor affordance: Unclear buttons and confusing file upload*

The file upload is cleaned up with a better affordance below (Figure 2-11). Drag and drop area is more obvious, cancel and upload buttons look more like buttons. Clear labeling of file size limits.

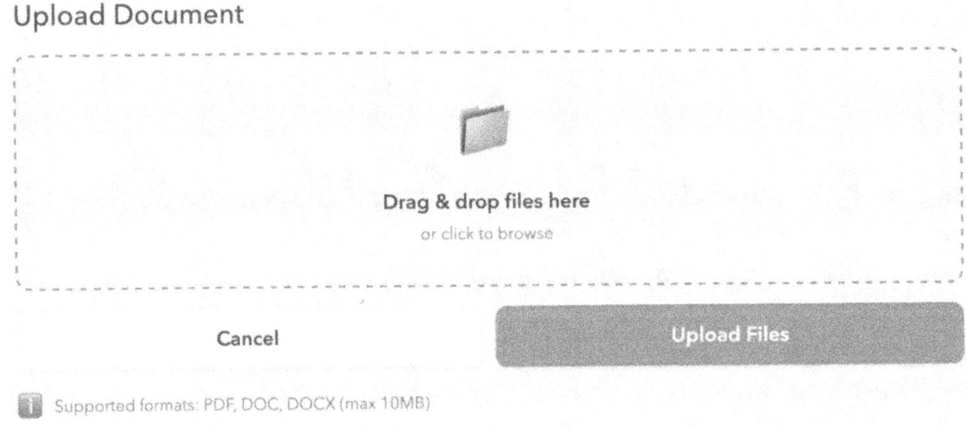

Figure 2-11. *Better affordance: Clear drag and drop area with obvious actions*

Context

To build great user experiences, we must understand where a user is coming from. We must understand if the user is coming in from a desktop or mobile device.

Hierarchy

The arrangement of items within a user interface element to indicate their importance and relationships. Much of what we create with our user experiences affects this. As an example, the placement of a search box on a page will affect how users expect this search box to behave.

- Size/Color/Contrast

- Spacing

- Placement

Figure 2-12 shows a confusing hierarchy example having multiple search buttons with unclear scope.

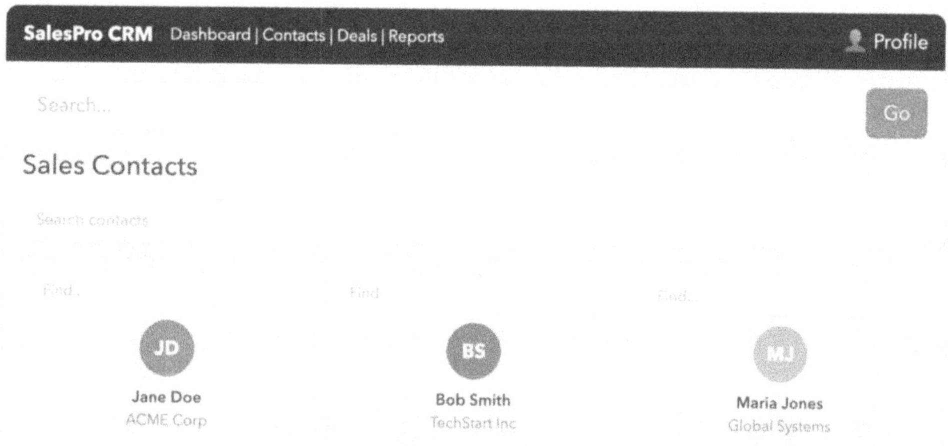

Figure 2-12. *Confusing hierarchy: Multiple search buttons with unclear scope*

A better hierarchy example is shown in Figure 2-13.

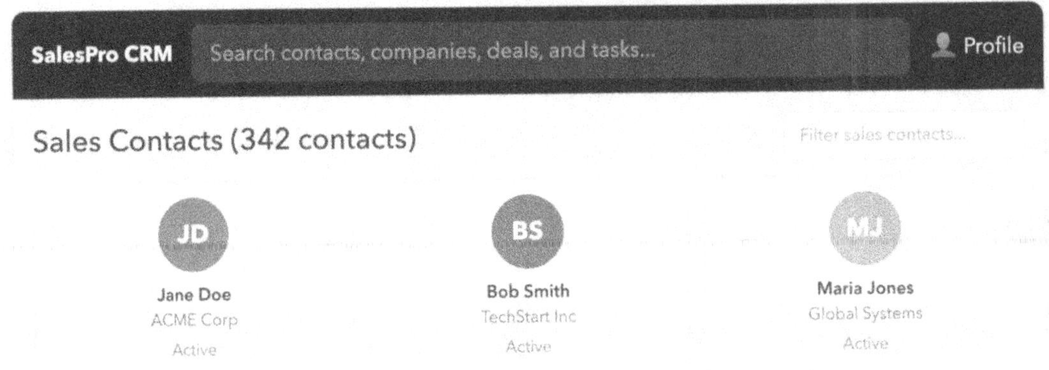

Figure 2-13. *Better hierarchy: Clear visual organization and single search*

Consistency

Uniformity in design elements and behavior in the user interface. Colors, typography, icons, and spacing need to be consistent within a user experience. Many user interfaces feel like the only thing consistent about them is that they are consistently inconsistent.

Figure 2-14 has many consistency problems. Inconsistent fonts, colors, and spacing make the following form almost difficult to look at.

Figure 2-14. *Consistency problems: Inconsistent fonts, colors, and spacing*

Figure 2-15 has better consistency. Font and colors are consistent for their purposes.

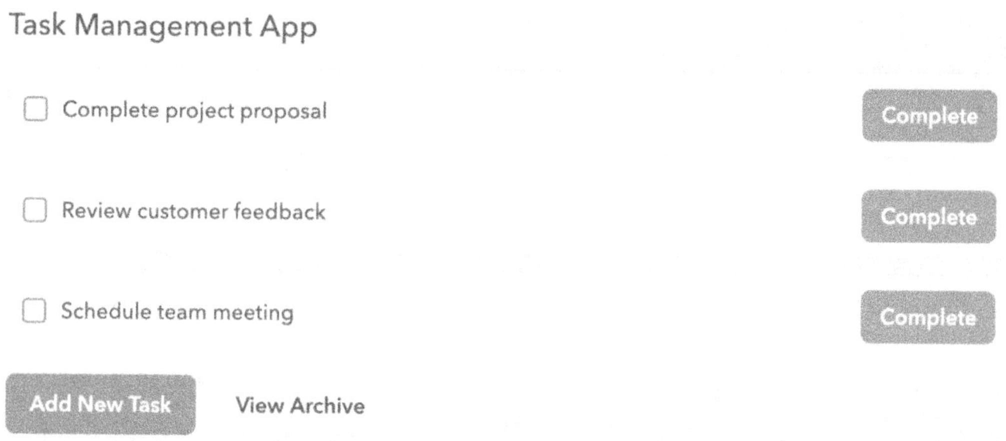

Task Management App

☐ Complete project proposal   Complete

☐ Review customer feedback   Complete

☐ Schedule team meeting   Complete

Add New Task   View Archive

Figure 2-15. *Better consistency: Uniform fonts, colors, and spacing*

Progressive Disclosure

Design should reveal complexity and functionality gradually, showing users only what they need at a given step. Doing this will reduce the mental complexity put upon the users, and allow users to ease into the software. And if we do this correctly, we can slowly reveal complexity and experts to shine using the software. As a core principle, start simple and reveal complexity as necessary.

Common techniques to achieve progressive disclosure:

- Expand/Collapse sections

- Multi-step wizards

- Inline expansion

- Tiered Interfaces (basic vs. advanced)

The example in Figure 2-16 has an "Advanced Options" button that will allow the user to access advanced features, if necessary.

Create Event

Event Name

Team Meeting

Date   **Time**

01/17/2026   12:30 PM

▶ ⚙ Advanced Options

Create Event

Figure 2-16. *Progressive disclosure: Advanced options revealed on demand*

Error Handling and Recovery

All systems will run into errors, and the better we can help users recover from these situations, the better. Obviously the better we can prevent errors the better, but if we can detect problems and show good errors to the user that can help us keep the user from getting frustrated.

The example below is for a good sign-up form. The user is given clear error messages describing why the email address is not valid, and why the password is not valid. These clear error messages make it easier for the user to resolve the errors and create their account.

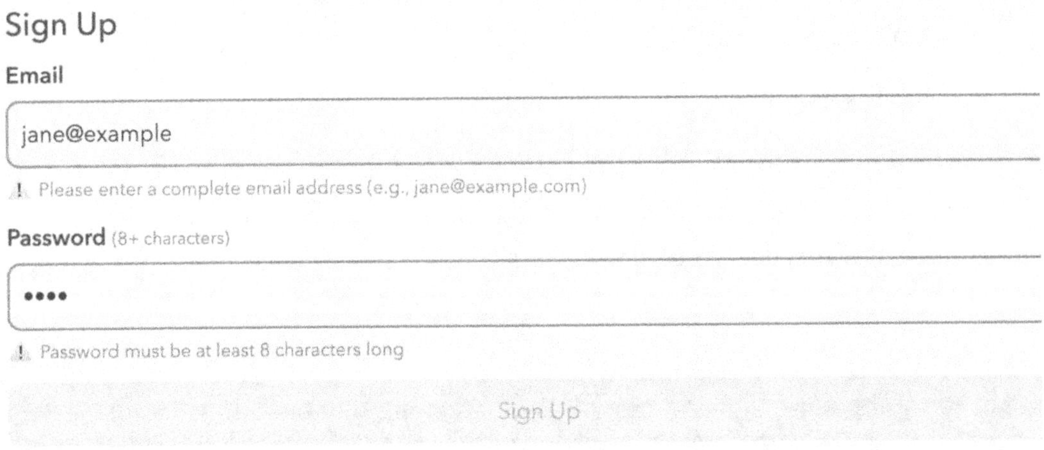

Sign Up

Email

jane@example

⚠ Please enter a complete email address (e.g., jane@example.com)

Password (8+ characters)

••••

⚠ Password must be at least 8 characters long

Sign Up

Figure 2-17. *Error handling: Clear error messages guiding user recovery*

The Triad—Novice, Developer, Power User

A common paradigm for thinking about users is three personas. The novice, the developer, and the power user. These personas are obvious, but let's go through them in a little more detail to make sure we are aligned.

The novice represents the non-tech-savvy people, occasional users of the software. These users need good affordance, things need to look exactly like what they expect. Nothing hidden, no special gestures, minimize requiring discovery to complete tasks.

Novice's failure signals:

- Where do I click?

- Gets lost

- Afraid to tap/click for fear of breaking it

- Calls support after 30 seconds

The developer persona represents the programmers, the sys admins, data analysts, and anyone who lives in terminals or spreadsheets. These users are often keyboard-first, with shortcuts being important. They prefer the ability to customize the experience and often prefer dark themes. They like dense information, tables, logs. The developer will prefer fast loading or nice animations.

Developer failure signals:

- Why can't I use keyboard navigation?

- Where is the bulk action/export / API?

- Why does this take three clicks?

- I need to see the actual data.

The power user (domain expert) is someone who uses a product for 8 hours a day. They are experts at that product. Knowing every menu and every setting. Muscle-memory focused—minimal friction on repetitive tasks. Power users will often rebel if things are changed.

Power user failure signals:

- Why is it still four clicks?

- Why did you move that button?

- Can't I just use the old version?

The big issue with these personas is that making all three happy with a user interface is difficult. Typically, it is assumed you can make two of these three user types happy. You can create a user experience that makes grandmas and developers happy, but not power users. You can create user interfaces that make developers and power users happy, but not grandmas. You can create user interfaces that make grandmas and power users happy, but not developers. Trying to make all three happy is very difficult. And often when we try to make all users happy, we make no one happy.

The following table describes many products and how they probably seem from these three personas.

Product	Novice	Developer	Power user	Verdict ($\geq$2)	Why
VS Code	2	5	5	Dev + PU	Built by/for devs; massive extensibility and keyboard focus.
Notion	4	3	4	Novice + PU	Clean and forgiving start.
Figma (2026)	3	4	5	Dev-ish + PU	Collaborative and fast for pros; learning curve for beginners.
MS Word (Ribbon)	4	2	4	Novice + PU	Ribbon helps with discoverability. Devs hate mouse-heavy.
Clippy (Office 97)	1	1	1	Fails all	Annoying popup. Difficult to escape. Hard to get value from.

There is a natural conflict or tension when trying to make all of these users happy. What will feel comfortable to a novice will feel slow to a developer. Customization and powerful UI are what power users want, but novices will want simplified experiences.

Figure 2-18 is an example of a user experience that is good for both grandmas and power users. The user interface is simple, with clear buttons, but it does allow for some advanced features.

Simple Photo Editor

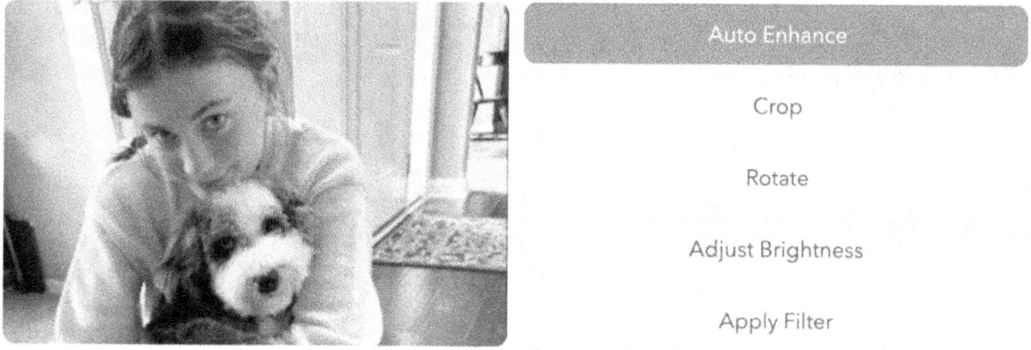

Figure 2-18. *User interface optimized for novice and power user personas*

In Figure 2-19 is another version of the user interface, we are favoring developers and power users. Here, we have some advanced controls, with fine-level control available.

Advanced Photo Editor

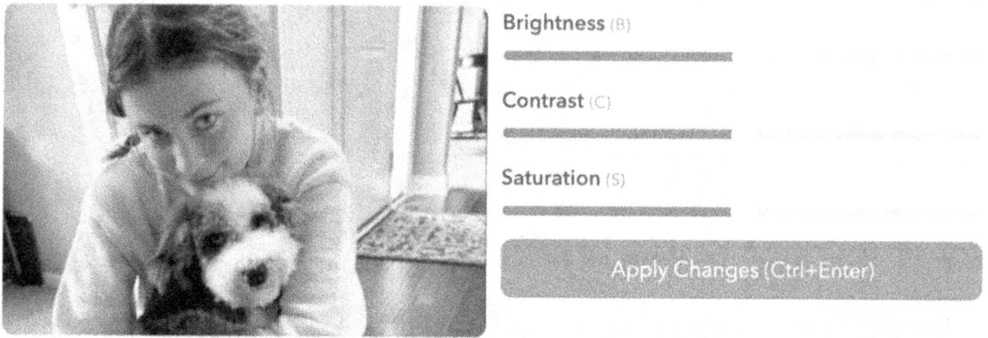

Figure 2-19. *User interface favoring developers and power users*

In this last example (Figure 2-20), we provide a version that fits for novices and developers. There are clear keyboard actions for the developers, and the actions are simpler, and easier for a novice user to understand.

Photo Quick Fix

Figure 2-20. *User interface balancing grandma and developer needs*

Each version is optimized for a different user group. Creating a version of this for all three of these users would be difficult. And we should try to build user experiences that are as usable as possible, but we must know our user group, or the users of this system. Trying to optimize for everyone will ultimately have us building a user interface that is optimized for no one, and everyone will be unhappy.

User Interface Component

User interfaces are composed of many components. Most of these components have been around since the early days of HTML. But some, such as video and canvas, are more recent additions.

- User interface elements

- Forms

- Input controls

- Labels

- Buttons

- Navigation

- Containers

- Informational

- Video

- Canvas

Forms

Forms are a collection of input fields and buttons that allow users to submit changes to data.

Examples:

- Signup/signin

- Contact/feedback

- Data entry

- Search

Figure 2-21 is an example lead create form.

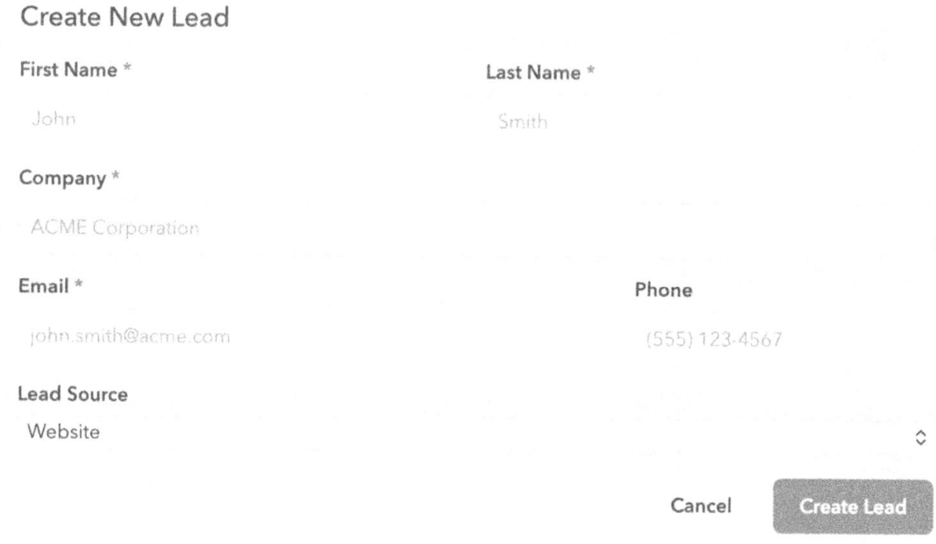

Figure 2-21. *Example lead creation form with input fields*

Input Controls

Input controls are the components that allow users to enter, select, and manipulate data. These controls are well known and used by users of all systems. Figures 2-22 and 2-23 show many of these input controls in use on a Contact Preferences form and on a Schedule Follow-Up form.

Input control types:

- Text Input (single and multi-line)

- Selection (dropdowns, radio buttons, checkboxes)

- Date/Time (Date pickers, time selection)

- Numeric (number inputs, steppers)

- File (file upload controls)

- Toggles (Switches)

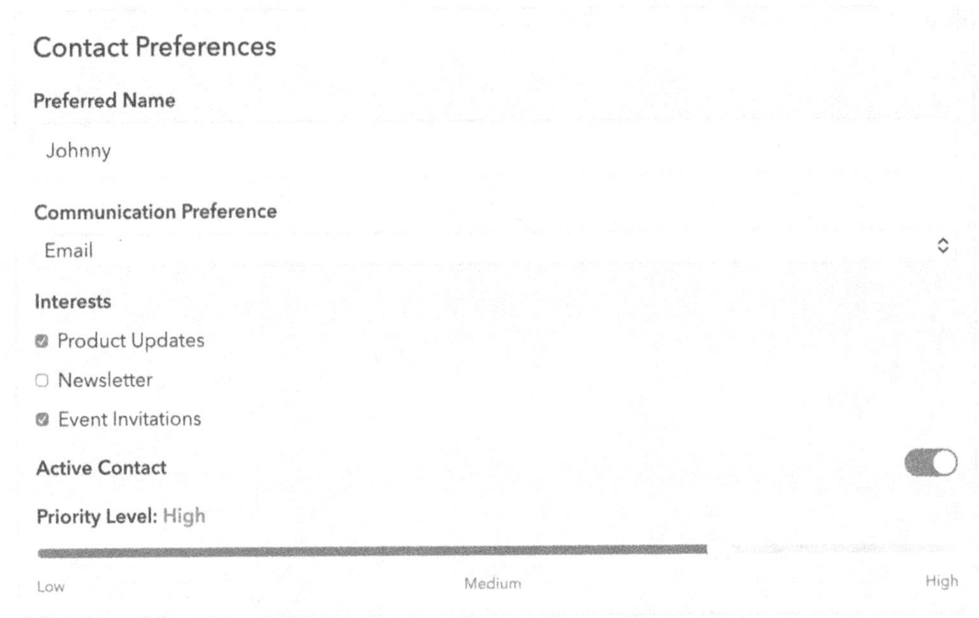

Contact Preferences

Preferred Name

Johnny

Communication Preference

Email

Interests

☑ Product Updates

☐ Newsletter

☑ Event Invitations

Active Contact

Priority Level: High

Low   Medium   High

Figure 2-22. Various input control types for data entry

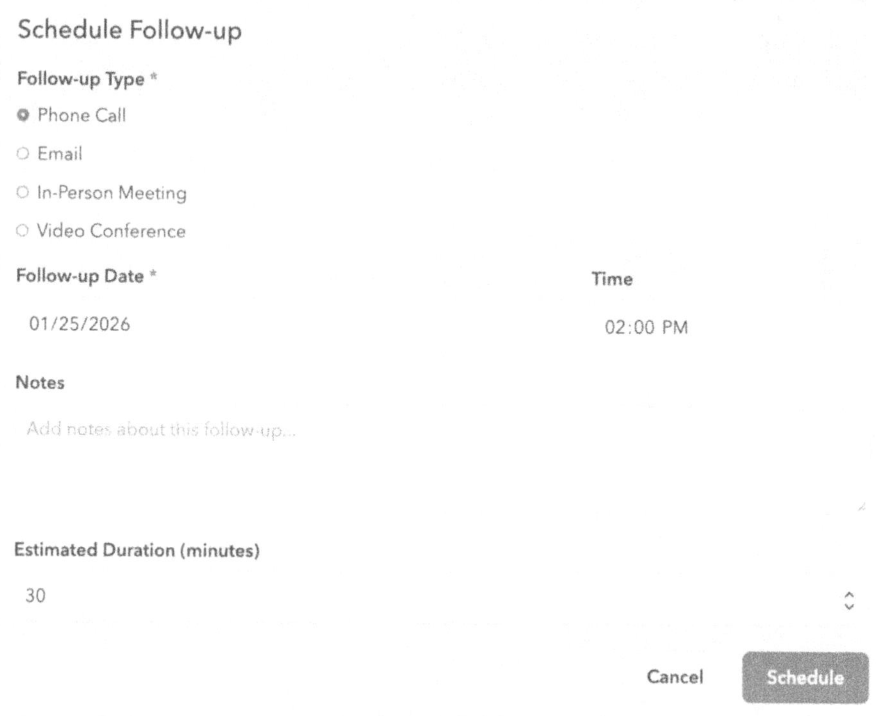

Schedule Follow-up

Follow-up Type *

● Phone Call

○ Email

○ In-Person Meeting

○ Video Conference

Follow-up Date *

01/25/2026

Time

02:00 PM

Notes

Add notes about this follow-up...

Estimated Duration (minutes)

30

Cancel   Schedule

Figure 2-23. *Additional input control examples*

Buttons

If input controls are how users enter data into a system, usually buttons are the clickable actions to submit the data. Buttons usually signify an action the system will perform for the user.

Most interfaces rely on a small, consistent set of button types so people always know what to expect. Primary buttons are the big, prominent ones that represent the main call to action on a page, the single most important thing you want the user to do, like "Save," "Submit," or "Continue." Secondary buttons handle less critical actions, such as going back, canceling, or choosing an alternative option. Many systems also include Danger buttons for actions that are hard or impossible to undo, like deleting an account or removing important data. These are usually styled differently (often red) to make users pause and think twice before clicking.

Getting these button distinctions right ties directly into WCAG principles. When buttons are clearly perceivable, properly labeled, and operable by keyboard or assistive tech, they help make interfaces more understandable for everyone. If you're not intentional about how these elements work across experience levels, you risk confusing people or creating barriers that leave some users out. Figure 2-24 shows a few of these button types.

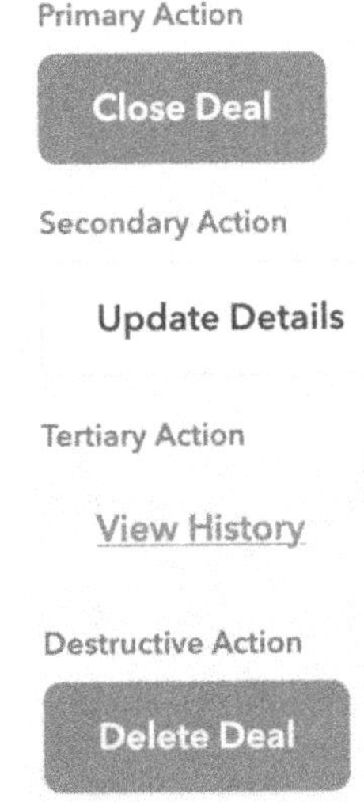

Figure 2-24. *Button styles and action controls*

Navigation

Most systems have multiple pages within the application. Each page usually has a different goal. Navigation elements allow the user to move from different pages (or subcomponents) within an application.

The following image shows many types of navigation in a single image. We have high-level navigation across the top, with breadcrumb navigation underneath. Then we have tab navigation showing Overview, Activity, Deals, and Documents. Figure 2-25 shows an example of navigation within a CRM system.

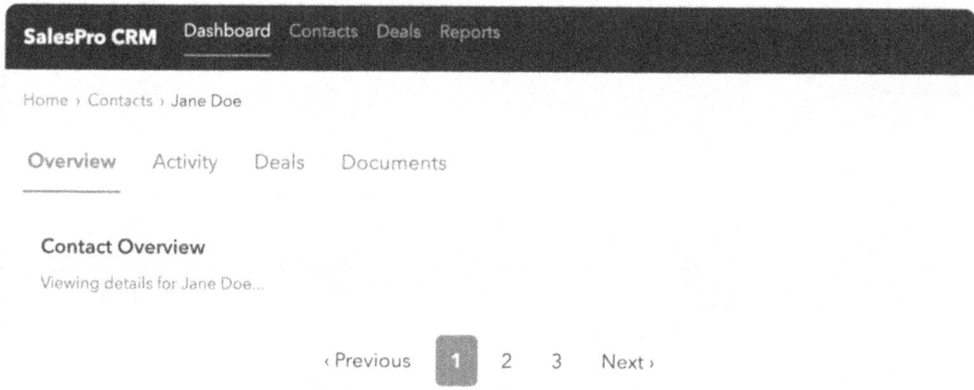

Figure 2-25. *Navigation components for multi-page applications*

Containers

Our user interfaces are more complex than a few fields and buttons. We need to create some structure within the pages. We usually do this by creating containers for visual elements.

Common containers:

- Cards

- Panels

- Modals/Dialogs

- Accordions

- Dividers

- Grids/Lists

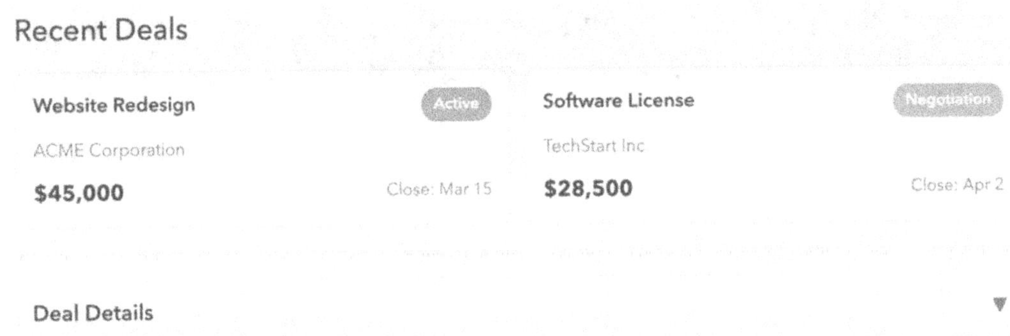

Figure 2-26. *Container components for organizing interface elements*

Informational

Informational components aid users in understanding what is going on. They often provide feedback or guide users.

Example informational components:

- Alerts/notifications
- Tooltips
- Badges
- Progress indicators
- Empty states
- Help text

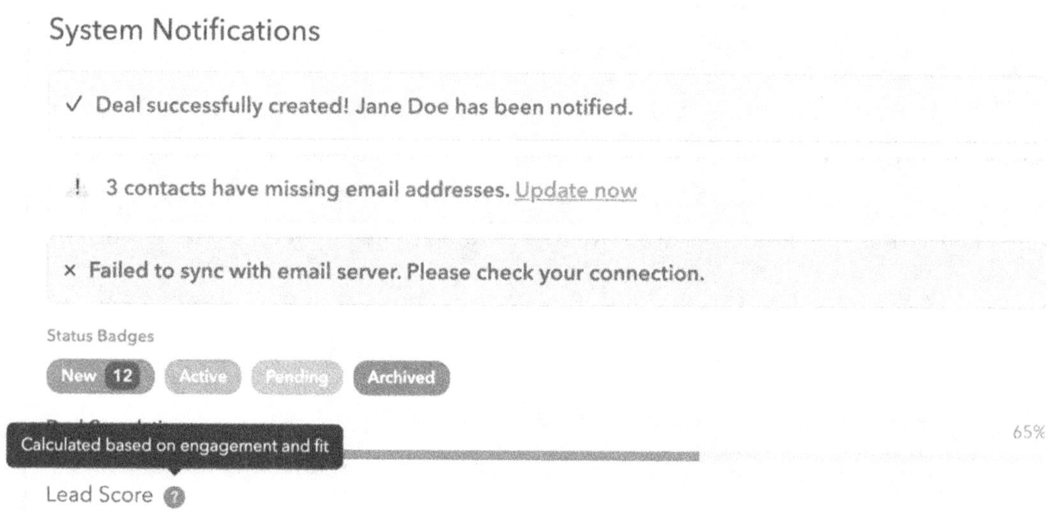

Figure 2-27. *Informational components for user guidance*

UI Design Decisions

How can we avoid cycling and arguing about what is the best user experience? This is maybe the real challenge in user experience. Everyone is a user experience expert; we all use interfaces daily, and we all have informed opinions. However, not all opinions are equal. User preference can be measured through usability testing and user feedback a more reliable foundation for decision-making.

How can we think differently, or break this cycle? Socratic method (Socrates 5 Questions) is a powerful way to think about user experience. With these questions, we can break apart our opinions and have a more analytical discussion. Here, I have created a synthesis from Socrates and the book *The Thinker's Guide to the Art of Socratic Questioning*, but with more of a focus on user experience.

The five question types we should be asking about the following categories:

- Clarification/definition

- Assumptions and belief

- Evidence and reason

- Alternative viewpoints

- Implications and consequences

This can be used in one of two ways. The first is during a design review. Instead of people stating that they don't like this button, the reviewers can only ask Socratic-style questions. The designer has to answer. The questions should be open-ended, probably non-judgmental. The following are potential reviewer questions for a user experience:

- What is the goal? (Clarification)

- What assumptions are we making? (Assumptions)

- Is this design decision grounded or a whim? (Evidence)

- What if we designed this differently? (Alternative)

- What are the downstream effects? (Implications)

The second way this can be used is after users struggle with a user experience. We can ask similar questions to learn why the user struggled.

Both of the options get us thinking about the user experience in an analytical way, and can remove some of the emotion common to these discussions, and that shift alone tends to produce better outcomes. Also, I think it is always important to focus on the last of the categories, what are the implications and consequences of this decision? Asking that question out loud often dissolves hours of debate. Consider how often we argue over a design decision, if we would just ask, what are the real consequences? We often realize the argument wasn't worth having in the first place.

Summary

In this chapter, we went the core building blocks of user interfaces, forms, inputs, controls, and buttons. We also learned why user interface design is far more complicated than most people realize. There are constant trade-offs between clarity, efficiency, and simplicity. When factoring in these trade-offs, it is important to realize that there is no perfect solution for all users; we are balancing creating user interfaces for many users and user types. Getting these fundamentals right sets the foundation for interfaces that work for novices, developers, and power users.

Key Takeaways

- Forms, controls, and buttons are the primary tools for user interaction, and their design affects users' ability to complete their goals.

- Clarity in visual hierarchy and affordance helps users understand what actions are available.

- Good error handling guides users toward solutions and can prevent problems from occurring.

- Accessibility standards like WCAG provide a foundation for building interfaces that work for everyone.

Bibliography

Paul, Richard, and Linda, Elder. (2006). *The Thinker's Guide to the Art of Socratic Questioning: Based on Critical Thinking Concepts & Tools.* Foundation for Critical Thinking.

CHAPTER 3

Conversations

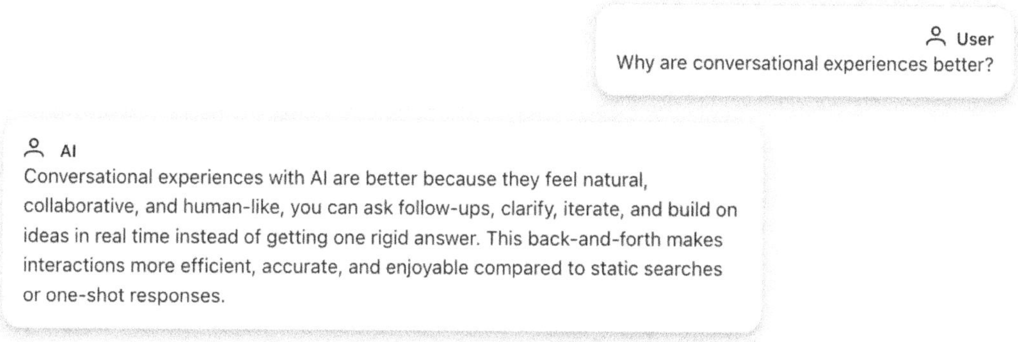

Figure 3-1. *AI describing why conversational experiences can improve human/ computer interaction*

Figure 3-1 provides a good response as to why conversational experiences can be better for users. Conversations can drastically change these interfaces. This chapter will describe the revolution that is occurring, the change from classic forms, controls, and buttons to conversations. This chapter will also describe where these changes will most benefit your application. The notion of conversational experiences has always been appealing. Conversations are more appealing than a complex user experience, more approachable and friendlier. But they were incredibly difficult to build. We have tried to create these solutions before LLMs, and they often resulted in horrible tree navigation structures. Figure 3-2 shows a classic choice selection option for chat.

C. Michel, *From Buttons to Conversations*, https://doi.org/10.1007/979-8-8688-2688-7_3

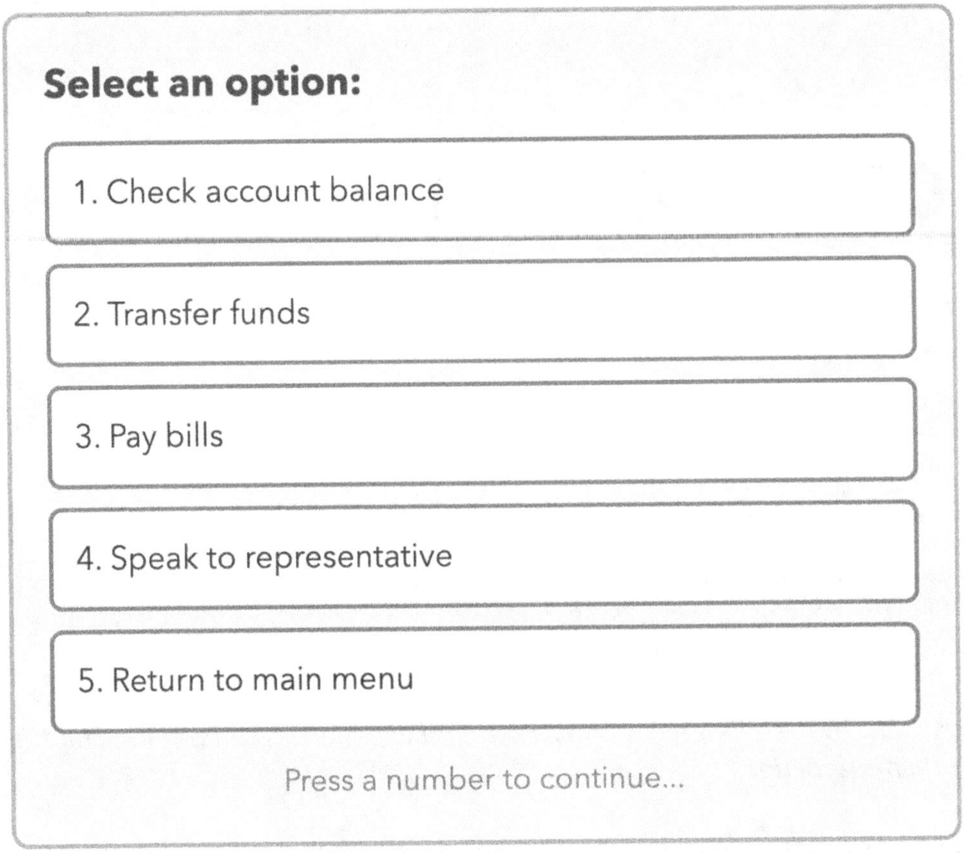

Select an option:

1. Check account balance

2. Transfer funds

3. Pay bills

4. Speak to representative

5. Return to main menu

Press a number to continue...

Figure 3-2. Traditional decision tree navigation in pre-LLM chatbots

A classic example of this was Microsoft's Clippy. Clippy was a cute concept. A paper clip would pop up and help you solve problems while working on a Microsoft Office document. Clippy had the appearance of a conversation, but unfortunately, it was more of a tree.

Clippy would pop up when you are trying to complete a task, offer to help, but leave you more frustrated. These interruptions rarely led to better outcomes. Help needs to be helpful, and Clippy was not.

From the Clippy failure, what should we take away? First, decision trees are very difficult to correctly create. I don't think these are impossible to create, but very difficult. Second, if you pop up and interrupt a user, solving the user's problem is essential.

The first problem is something LLMs are great at solving. People can communicate with these assistants in natural language, instead of trying to correctly navigate a tree, something we users quickly realize we are trying to do. The second problem, actually solving the problem, is a very difficult problem too. We will discuss some solutions to this in Chapter 4 but realize that we can't just have a great conversation around the problem. We must build assistants that are actually useful.

LLMs gave us natural language understanding and the ability to respond in natural language. We no longer have to build these decision trees. We can enable users to navigate through a conversation. Figure 3-3 shows a chat interface driven by an LLM with no decision tree.

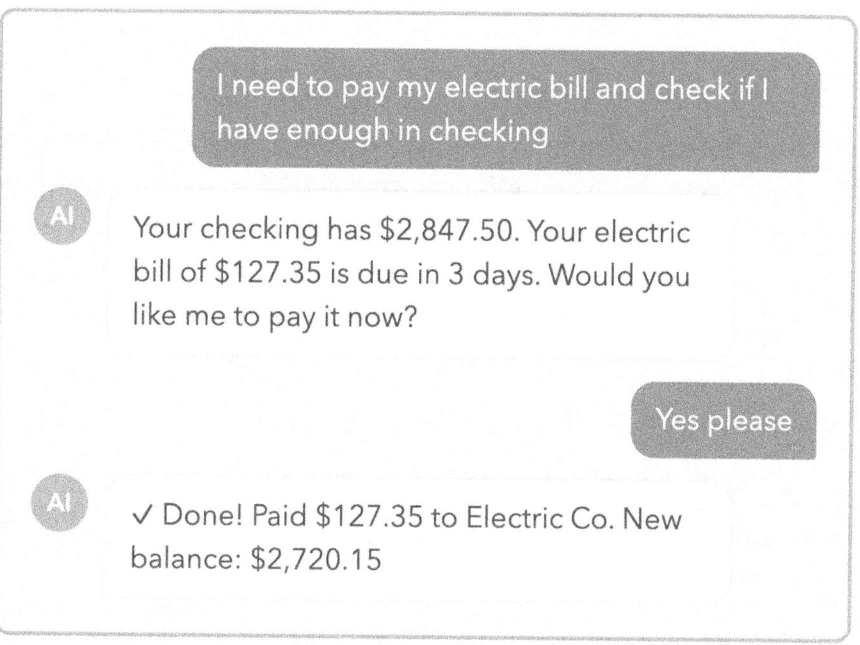

Figure 3-3. *LLM-powered natural language conversation interface*

This change to user experience is aligned with how we want to interact with computers. Forms and buttons were always about bridging the gap between users and computers. Now with modern LLMs, the gap can grow closer, with users just telling the computer what they want done. Buttons provided a safety net with potential validation before performing a task.

This Agentic conversation revolution will allow to better create user interfaces that understand natural language, remember context across conversations, and take actions on behalf of users, learn more interactions over time, and adapt to users' needs.

As we consider the implications of moving toward conversational experiences, let's revisit the aspects of user experience we discussed in Chapter 2.

Aspects of User Experience Revisited

Moving to a conversational experience does not mean we no longer care about the same aspects of user experience. In this section, we will see some of the advantages (and some disadvantages) of conversational experiences.

Usability

Conversations are the normal mode for human-to-human interaction, so extending that to human-to-computer is an easy extension. A conversational user interface doesn't require a big learning curve. Almost all users will be at home with a conversational experience, and they will be pleasantly surprised when your user experience is actually helpful. Figure 3-4 shows an example of a conversational experience.

Advantages:

- No complex user interface to learn.

- Efficiency, no navigation required.

- Error prevention; AI can ask clarifying questions to prevent ambiguous operations.

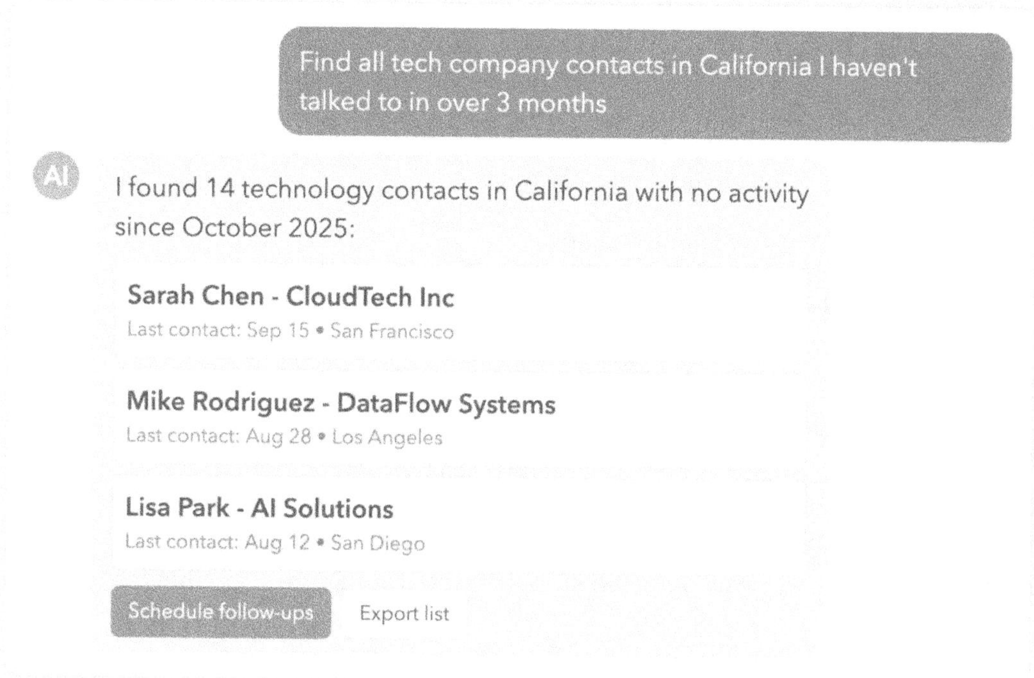

Figure 3-4. Conversational UX demonstrating usability advantages

Accessibility

As we talked before, accessibility is extremely important and a legal requirement. One of the problems with our more and more extensive user interfaces is that they are often made less accessible.

The great thing about conversations is that at their core, conversations are text. Screen readers will process conversations great, and since we are limiting the controls to just a button and some text, screen readers should provide a great experience for these conversations.

While accessibility should be a no-brainer with conversations, we often create "thinking" or "processing text." This text could be confusing for a screen reader. To avoid making this read to a blind user, we should use an aria-hidden attribute on this text. Just because conversations are mostly text doesn't guarantee that we will be more accessible, we have to make sure we don't mess it up.

Advantages:

- Screen readers should naturally work.

- No precise motor control is required to use.

- Natural language has a low cognitive load.

- Auditory text-based alternative.

- Multi-language AI can translate and adapt in real time.

Affordance

Conversations have a big advantage here. Since the user will be focused on the conversation and on the recent response. Making things discoverable and easy to understand is very possible. Figure 3-5 shows an agent suggesting possible responses.

Advantages:

- AI can suggest what is possible.

- Prompts can clarify when needed.

- The system can show sample queries to use.

- An agent can provide quick acknowledgements.

I want to create a deal

AI I can help you create a deal! I'll need a few details. What's
the company name?

Or try: "Create a deal for ACME Corp worth $50K closing next
month"

TechFlow Industries

AI Great! What's the deal value?

$10K-$25K $25K-$50K $50K-$100K $100K+

Figure 3-5. *Conversation shows good affordance as potential responses provided inline*

Context

A lot of existing user interfaces do a great job with context, if the user knows what to look for. But if the user doesn't use the software very often, those contextual clues can be difficult to pick up on.

This is another area where a simplified context is easier to follow, especially for users who do not use software frequently. With familiar tools, an experienced user barely thinks about the interface, they just work. But you throw me into an editor I am not familiar with, I'll probably struggle a little to get my bearings. The ability to ask a question, "how do I debug and set a breakpoint," could be very powerful in those situations. Figure 3-6 shows how context can be used to help answer future questions.

Advantages:

- Remember the current conversation.

- An agent can know users' preferences.

- Track multistep workflows.

- An agent can understand time, location, and urgency.

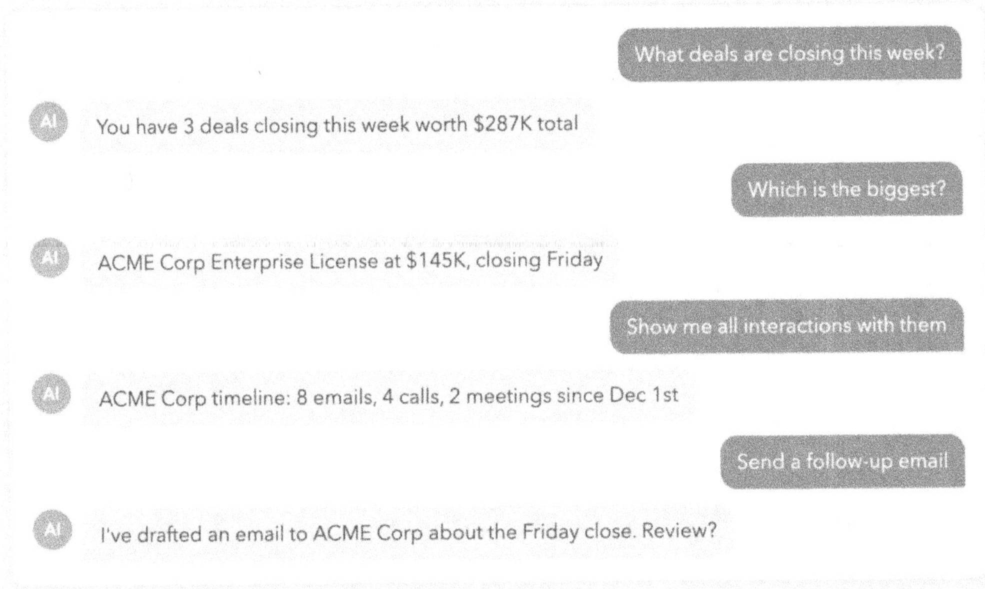

Figure 3-6. *AI agent using context from current conversation to answer future questions*

Consistency

Conversational experiences are by their nature often constrained to almost a request/response model. User asks a question, and the agent responds. This should create a lot of consistency for the user, the user experience never changes.

Advantages:

- Minimal UI to learn

- Common and repeated pattern

- Same voice

- Predictable feature set

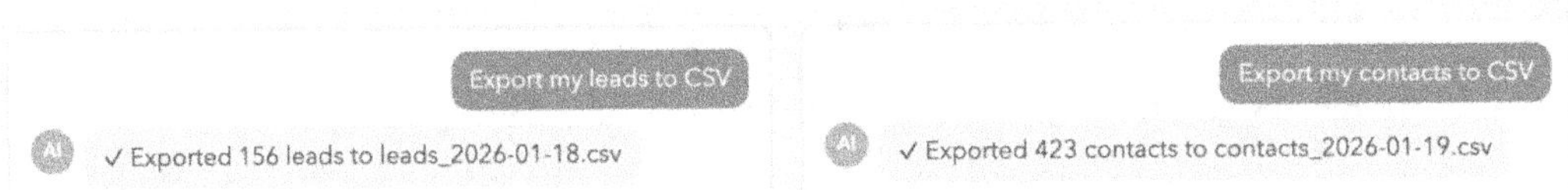

Figure 3-7. *Consistency in response. Two similar actions result in similar responses*

It is important that our conversations are consistent, allowing users to almost predict the response. Keeping the responses simple and consistent will help users feel comfortable with these new interfaces. Figure 3-7 shows how consistency can be maintained in conversations.

Being extremely simple, text in and text out will only work for simple tasks. As our systems become more complex, simple text interfaces often are not the ideal way to interact with data. We will want to build in more complex options, and that is where Progressive Disclosure comes in.

Progressive Disclosure

Progressive disclosure is the slow revealing of more features to users. This principle allows us to reveal more complexity to users, but only if needed or desired by the user. With a standard user experience, this could often be seen as an accordion. We allow the user to expand to see more information if they want.

In a conversational world, we have a lot of the same options available to us. We could use accordions within the chat to enable the user to look deeper into data, if they want. But conversations allow a couple of other ways to enable users to go deeper if they want. The first is by embedding links in our responses. These links could be to other parts of the system that have more information on the topic. The second is our agents can provide a limited amount of information, but ask, "would you like to know more?" And expand with more information only if the user wants us to dive deeper. Figure 3-8 shows the AI agent asking follow-up questions in the response.

We have all seen this done poorly, a user interface that shows us a lot of options right from the start. When this happens, we almost always realize that we are going to need some help to use this tool. As a software developer, I have always felt that developer tools are particularly bad at this. They show so many options that it is almost like they are trying to keep people away. Something is changing; many development tools are now showing a conversation as the starting point.

Advantages:

- More options available.

- AI can reveal features over time.

- Clarifying questions can be asked.

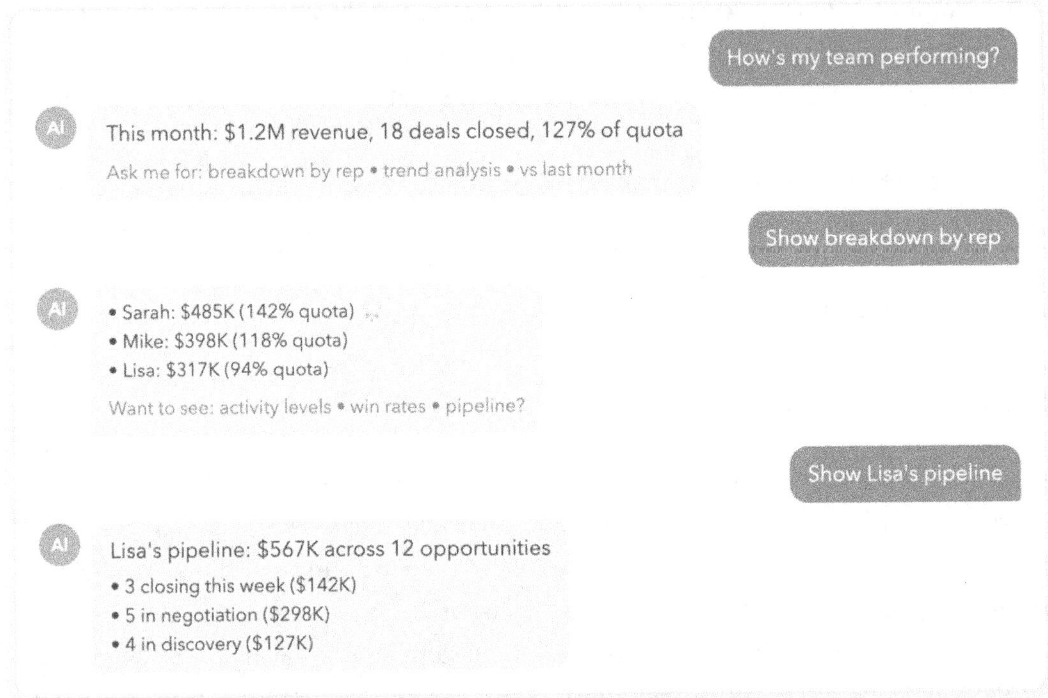

Figure 3-8. *Conversation provides hints at what to look into next: "Want to see: activity levels, win rates, pipelines?"*

Error Handling and Recovery

Anyone who has worked with software for a long time has probably experienced the "oh no, I just deleted …" moment. In these moments, we do something with software that is often difficult to recover from.

My situation where an agent could have saved me was in 2012 when I was uploading around terabytes of images into the cloud. The upload took a few days to complete. And we had a final process of finalizing the upload by writing a few database records into the database. Unfortunately for me, the button to wire it up in the database was right next to the button to delete the blob container (storage container in the cloud), and I clicked the wrong button. This button had no "Are you sure?". And I deleted a terabyte of images. That is why good error handling and recovery are important. An "Are you sure?" dialog would have saved me days of uploading images a second time. Figure 3-9 provides an example of a warning before deleting contacts.

A big advantage of working in conversations is that the agents can ask us those questions before we click the button. Now, a poorly implemented conversation system is no better than a poorly implemented forms/buttons system (like mentioned above). Still, AI can be an extra layer of analysis on our actions.

Advantages:

- AI can confirm before performing dangerous actions.

- Ask clarifying questions when uncertain.

- Easy to fix misunderstandings.

- AI agents can offer alternatives.

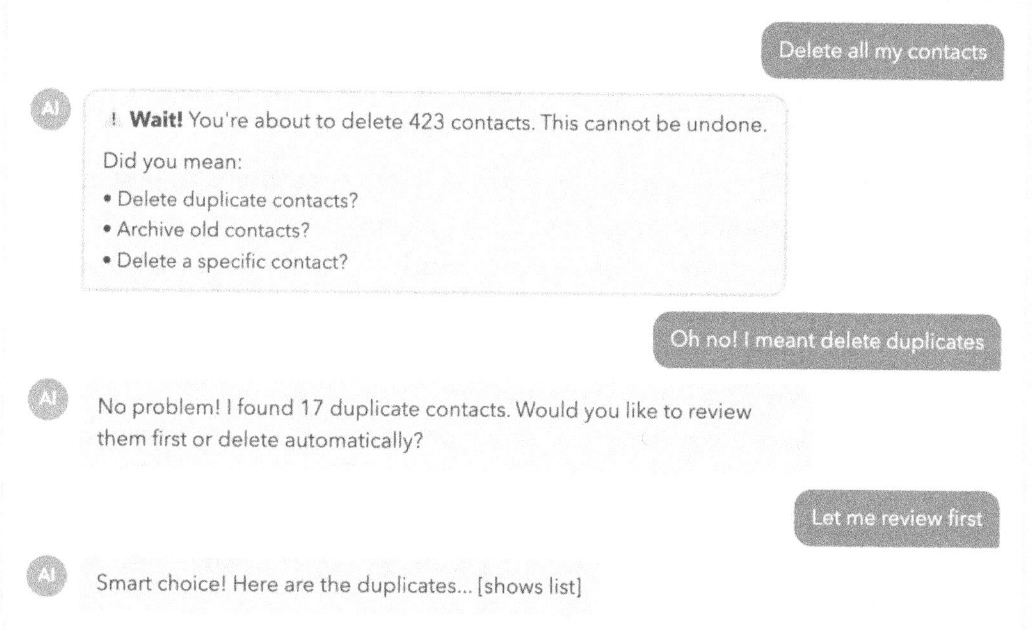

Figure 3-9. *A clear warning is provided before doing a destructive operation*

The Triad and Conversations

The Triad refers to three user personas: the novice, the developer, and the power user. The novice represents the user with low technical abilities. The developer has high technical skills, and wants a high level of control. The power user is more technical than the novice, but not as much as the developer. But the power user wants speed and efficiency more than anything else.

In Chapter 2, we discussed how it can be hard to optimize a user experience for these three user personas. We can optimize for the novice, but developers and power users will feel suffocated. We can optimize for the developer but the novice and power user want simpler interfaces. We can optimize for power users, but novices will find it hard to understand, and developers will want more control.

Attribute	Novice	Developer	Power User
Wants	Simplicity	Efficiency	Capability
Usage	Occasional	Frequent use	Regular use
Values	Clarity	Power	Features
Needs	Guidance	Speed	Features

The novice persona is a user who craves simplicity. They are probably best described as occasional users with low software experience. The novice persona is a user who has a task to complete, wants to complete it, but is okay with the software taking some liberties. A novice persona probably will not know exactly how they want a photo enhanced, but they might want it enhanced.

The developer persona is a user who wants efficiency and control. They probably know exactly what they want and will be disappointed if they can't get exactly what they want.

The nice thing about conversations is that they can be a win for all three of these users. Let's relook at how conversations can create happy novices, happy developers, and happy power users.

The novice doesn't want to know what "enhance" does, but she does have goals. She knows she needs the image enhanced before she can publish it. Maybe even crop it for publishing purposes. Figure 3-10 shows a good conversation of a novice updating a picture.

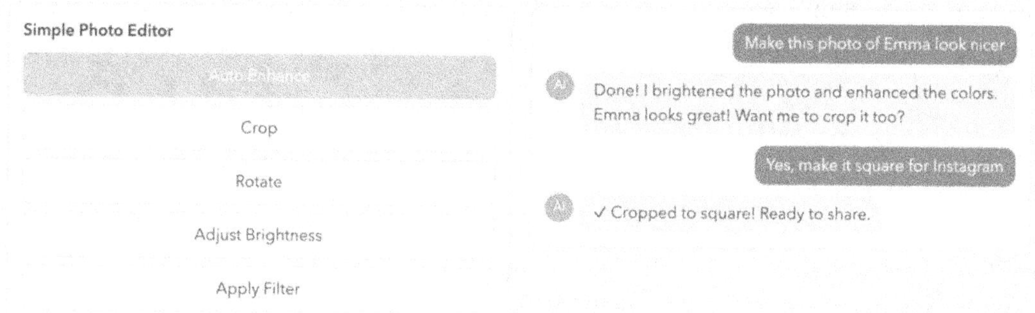

Figure 3-10. *Grandma persona: Simple conversational image editing*

Developer

The next persona is the developer. Developers want full control and the ability to complete their work quickly with precision. In the example below the developer can just change the brightness by telling the AI agent to increase brightness by 15. Figure 3-11 shows a conversation for the developer persona.

Figure 3-11. *Developer persona: Supports direct editing of values*

It might be hard to believe that developers will want to interact using a chat format instead of a tool with many buttons, big text areas, and a dark mode. But as of the time of this writing, many developers are spending more time interacting with AI agents than writing code.

Developers are often the early leaders on trends, and they are already using conversation first! Developers were one of the first to do remote work, which is now common. Developers jumped into bitcoin, and were some of the first big winners. Many developers were some of the first into biohacking. The nature of developers to be early to try things often puts them at the start of trends. And the trend in user interfaces is conversations.

Power User

Power users want the quick actions, things that are repeatable and consistent. In the example below, the power user is given quick buttons that enable predictable responses. The notion of giving users more than just text responses is a concept we will be discussing in detail in our next section. Figure 3-12 shows a conversation optimized for a power user.

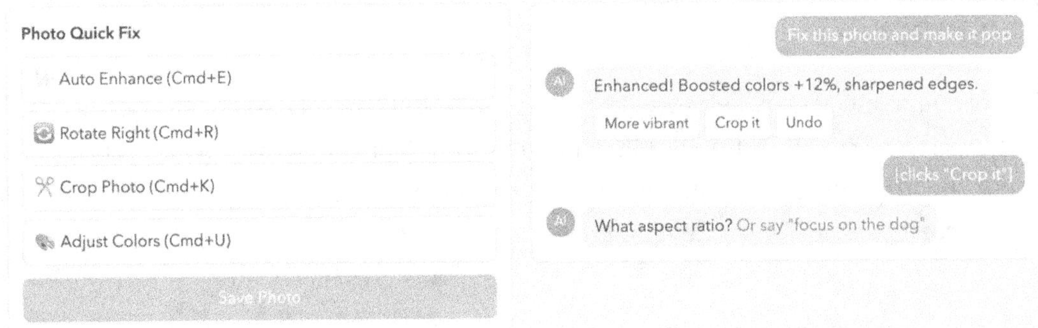

Figure 3-12. Power user persona, quick action buttons for efficiency

Power users might be the hardest group to convert to conversations, as they know their software extremely well and are very fast at using it. Power users will require things such as quick replies (covered in the next section) to ensure the software is fast and enables these users to continue to be efficient and get things done that they want quickly.

Eight Conversational Patterns

Building out these conversational interfaces isn't just a matter of building AI Agentic Chat into your application, we can do that, but just chat isn't going to be enough. We will want to create great conversational experiences; we can easily just create basic conversational experiences that are worse than forms and buttons.

Accessibility First

Maximizing the number of people who can use our applications is always important, and this new conversational interface gives us many advantages. The first of which is that we are mostly sending text back and forth, which should work great with screen readers.

Conversations provide us the ability to interact through pure conversation. Removing the need to create a custom user experience for a feature is a huge advantage. Plus, since we are not creating as much user experience, it is easier for us to ensure the user experience we do have is very accessible. Figure 3-13 shows a chat offering to allow voice input and audio output.

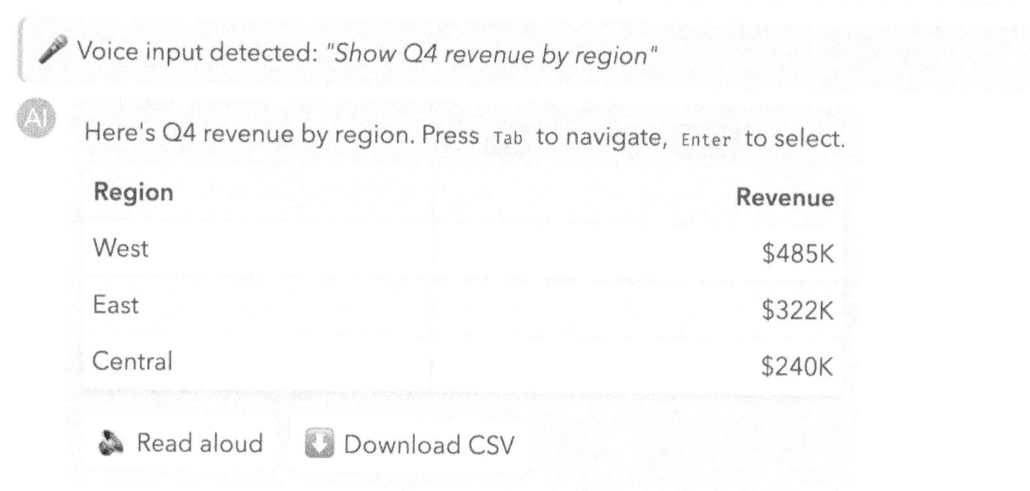

Figure 3-13. *Accessibility-first design with screen reader support*

Clear Turn-Taking

One potential issue with conversations is talking over each other. We have all experienced this in our real lives, and if we are not careful, we will build conversational systems that have similar issues.

With our conversational systems, we should know who is going to speak next. We want our conversations to be orderly and easy to follow. As we build our conversational user interfaces, we need to make sure the user knows when the system is responding and when the user can send another request. Most conversational systems disable the input text box and the send button while the AI Agent is responding. Figure 3-14 shows the text and send button as disabled while waiting for the AI agent to respond.

Figure 3-14. *Disabled input text and send button*

Part of clear turn-taking is having responses that encourage the next response. Ending a response with a clear question, if we expect the user to respond. In the example below, the agent ends with "Ready to proceed?", encouraging the user to respond with an affirmative, "yes." Figure 3-15 shows the agent asking a very clear question, and a ready to proceed message before performing an operation.

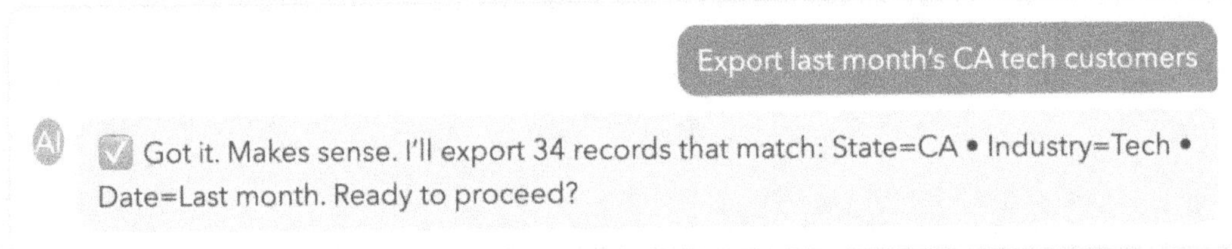

Figure 3-15. *Clear indication for the user to respond*

These little details are important for creating top-level user experiences. These details, such as disabling the text boxes or a clear request to respond to text, help to improve the affordance of the application and make the application easier to understand.

Token Streaming/Processing Indication

"Thinking" or some text like that is common as we build out these user experiences. This "thinking" text denotes that the agent is processing the request. A big reason this is necessary is that LLMs can be slow at times. Users expect fast responses, and LLMs can be slow enough that users will start wandering away.

Thinking is an option for displaying to users, but a "thinking" plus bouncing dots is not ideal for more than a second or so. If we are going to be paused for a few seconds, we should consider token streaming. With token streaming, we can begin to show the response before it completes. By showing this response before the LLM is finished, we can show some text back to the user. This allows the user to begin reading the response before it is finished. And if you are like me, you probably can't keep up with reading the text as it is streamed back, so this makes the LLM response seem very fast, faster than I can comprehend. Figure 3-16 shows an example of showing the "thinking" text.

When building out our conversational user interfaces, be careful not to make things less accessible. This thinking text can be a problem for screen readers. Be sure to hide the text with aria-hidden to prevent screen readers from reading this text to the user.

Token streaming can result in text being displayed to the user that is later changed. Changing text out from underneath a reader will be a lousy experience for users using a reader. In those situations, not displaying the text until it is completed would be the better option.

Figure 3-16. *Clear indication of agent processing*

"Thinking" is an okay default. It is clear and easy to understand. If your AI Agent could be in multiple states, we may want to consider changing the text to denote those states. "Thinking" could be our default, and we could change the text to "Waiting on external system," if we are waiting on a call from an external system for the agent to complete its work.

Some companies are having a little more fun with their "Thinking" text. Many development tools are cycling many more amusing statements while users wait. Choosing to do this does hurt your application's consistency, but it does make your agent feel a little more fun and playful. It might be worth trying and seeing if your users prefer it.

Quick Replies

The open-ended nature of conversations is, in some ways, great for software, but it can be difficult for users from two perspectives. First, it always requires some typing. Many users struggle to type, or maybe just prefer the mouse. Second, sometimes users will not know what to type. One advantage of a classic form user interface is that the user is often constrained.

Many times when interacting in a conversation, there are a few most likely responses. If the AI Agent asks a yes or no question, then a yes or no response makes the most sense. The quick replies are low effort, which allows users to just click a response instead of typing an entire response.

In the example below, the user is asked to confirm an action. The user could type "yes" as an affirmation. But if the user is using a mobile device, not a fast typer, or already using their mouse a quick click of "yes" will feel better.

Also, these quick replies are an excellent way to prompt users with potential other actions, such as "Review Template" or "Open Report." Both options are probably actions you might want to take before sending them an email.

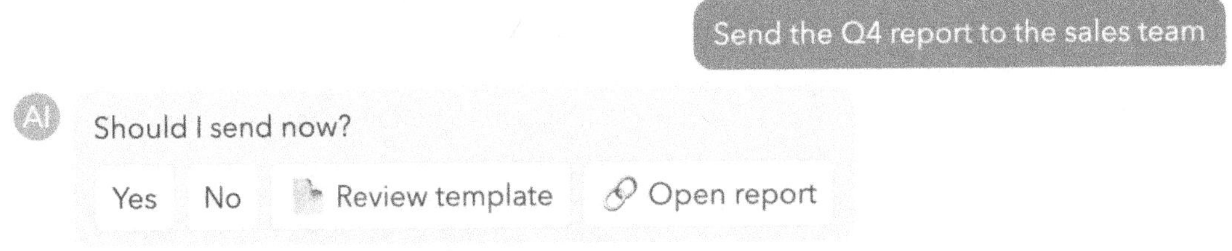

Figure 3-17. *Quick reply buttons for common responses*

Quick replies can often reveal features for the user, by hinting at other operations the user might want to do. In the previous example, the "Open Report" potentially opens another area of the software, effectively training the user on a new area of the software. This is a good use of the progressive disclosure concept mentioned before.

Sources

One of the most common objections to LLMs and AI Agents is the hallucination problem. LLMs will sometimes generate non-true text.

This problem can reveal itself in many subtle ways. The meme from a few years ago was how many r's are in strawberry. The correct answer is obviously 3, but many LLMs would confidently say 2. Which is part of the problem, LLMs seem to know everything, even things they don't know.

Now, the number of r's in strawberry isn't probably that important to know, but LLMs have been known to make up entire quotes.

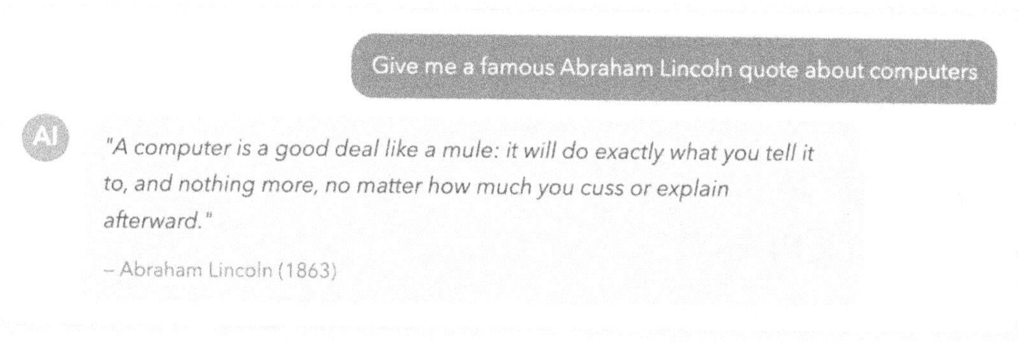

Figure 3-18. *LLMs can make up quotes*

These hallucinations are improving; we seem to get fewer and fewer of them. And most models can now answer "how many r's are in strawberry?" correctly. But we are far from 100% accurate. Figure 3-18 shows a conversation with a made-up quote demonstrating that AI can make up data.

Since users will be wary of responses from LLMs (and for good reason), we need to find a way to ground the responses. The easiest way to achieve this is when returning results, include links to the source material. If we are pulling information from the company policy document, include a link to that with our response. Even better would be to include a snippet of the relevant text so the user can easily verify the response. Figure 3-19 shows how a conversation agent can link to source documents to allow the user to verify the results.

Figure 3-19. *Source citations and tool references in responses*

In Chapter 4, we will discuss how grounded responses can be achieved. In that chapter, we will discuss RAG models and MCP (Model Context Protocol) as solutions to this problem.

When providing sources, be sure to remember the principle of information hierarchy. We will inform the user that the generated response comes from these sources. In the previous example, the Sources are listed under the response, clearly indicating that the response was generated from these sources.

Also, since the sources will be links, we will want to make them look like links within the application. Again, the principle of affordance is at play here. We will want it to be obvious that these are links the user can follow.

Persistent Context

Imagine if in each conversation you must retell all prior knowledge for it to be used in the conversation. With software, though, there is rarely a baseline. Every session typically starts from scratch, which means the user has to be re-establish context each time. That is a tax we have quietly accepted, but on that conversational AI can finally eliminate This baseline is somewhat context-dependent. If I meet someone from my home state while traveling in a different state, we can probably immediately begin talking about our state's football team. It will feel like we are jumping into a conversation that is going on with the entire state joining in.

When talking to a co-worker about a project we are both involved in, it would be natural for both of us to almost assume we are starting our conversation where it left off. Working with a computer is sometimes exhausting, because they don't really remember much about us or our goals. Each time we come back, we are starting over.

With classical forms systems, this starting over was annoying, but not much worse than annoying. Because each form was a separate navigation, and often we were performing the next tasks every few minutes, it probably wasn't a big issue. But as we move into conversations, persistent context becomes a bigger and bigger issue.

Figure 3-20. *Persistent context remembering conversation history*

By using context, a lot of answers can be provided without requiring the user to type in those answers. In the example above, context is used to schedule for the user's preferred time of 10 AM. Figure 3-20 shows an example using a user's preferred time for a meeting.

Context can be pulled from the conversation itself. If a user recently created a contact. Then, tells the agent to add that contact to an event, the system should be capable of pulling the recent contact from the conversation. The user shouldn't have to provide the recently created contact's information (or ID) to get the system to assign the contact to an event.

Rich Response/Dynamic Forms

We have built increasingly complicated user experiences partially because we needed to. Conversation can help reduce that complexity a lot, but sometimes more advanced visuals can really help.

Text is useful for conversations, but the communication of some concepts will be better in a richer format. Communication of complex or structured information will be easier in tables or charts.

Tables make it easier for side-by-side comparisons, such as pricing information, flight options, or performance metrics. A chart can instantly reveal trends, proportions, or changes over time.

Richer responses allow for quick comprehension and decision-making. Humans can process three bar charts faster than looking at a bunch of numbers in text. These richer responses can reduce the "which one is higher questions."

Richer responses are a must if we want to be conversation-first experiences. Almost all systems will need to present numbers or trends back to the user. Trying to explain those trends in plain text is difficult, a quick table or chart will reduce the cognitive load on the user, and make your conversation experience better. Figure 3-21 shows an example of a dynamic form embedded within a conversation.

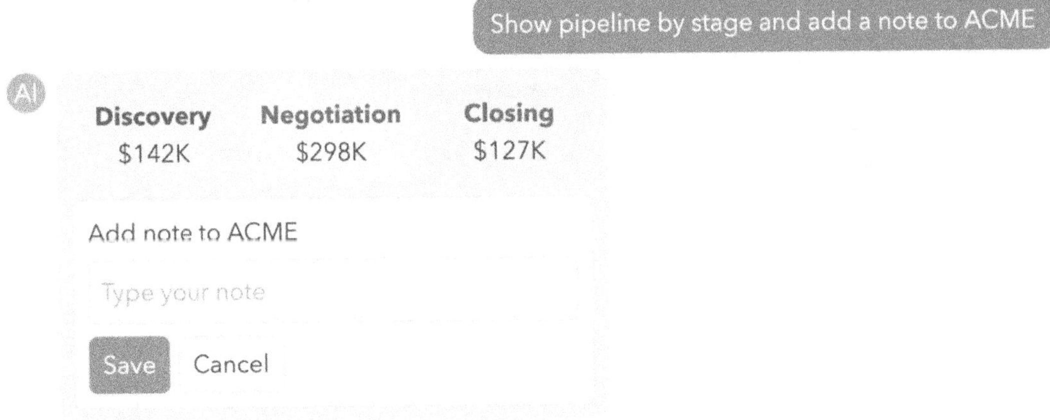

Figure 3-21. *Rich response with embedded table data*

Multi-modal and Long Memory

Much of what is covered in this book does have good examples in the world today, but this is not really here yet. Conversations with computers are still somewhat tied to the device associated with the conversation. There are counterexamples to my statement, but by and large, we are still managing the chats with these systems.

And if we start our conversation in text, we will usually stay in a text conversation. Voice conversations tend to be voice conversations. This is again because we are managing the conversations, we are not conversing with a single true agent.

Assuming we are conversing with an agent for a CRM system. We use our desktop to create a new contact "Bob". We then try to send an email to this new contact asking for a meeting, but our email system is down. The way these agent systems work now, we would be required to come back later and ask the agent to send an email to "Bob" to set up the meeting.

And if we came in from another device, or maybe called into the agent, the system would have no knowledge of this previous conversation. We would almost have to tell agent to again send the email to "Bob" to set up a meeting. This isn't the way we would interact with a person.

If we couldn't set up a meeting, the next time we saw the person, we would ask, can we set up the meeting now? And the person would again try and set up the meeting. But that really isn't the way the conversation would work. People have memories and can continue to perform tasks while we are not interacting with them. A person would continue to try to schedule the meeting even though we are not constantly chatting with them, they would continue to work in the background. And the best part of this scenario is that the next time we see this person, they will tell us that the meeting with Bob has been scheduled. Our agents must get to this level of autonomy. That said, autonomy without accountability is a risk. Any agent acting on a user's behalf should maintain a clear approval trail, letting users review, confirm, or override actions before they are executed.

True multi-modal conversations with agents will become a thing. And once it happens, computers will feel so much more useful.

Designing for multiple modalities means your interface should degrade gracefully depending on how the user is engaging. A voice assistant needs to compress information into shorter, sentences that can be spoken, not tables, no links. A visual interface can use charts and structured responses. A mobile device might lean on quick replies and minimal typing. The best agentic systems will detect modality and adapt accordingly. Figure 3-22 shows an AI agent offering to send a conversation to a mobile device.

Voice interfaces in particular deserve careful attention. When a user speaks to an agent, the turn-taking dynamic shifts, there is no send button, no visible chat history, and not quick-reply chips. The agent has to manage the pace of the conversation and adapt to the user. The agent may have to use prompts like "I'm ready" to engage the user to reply. All of this means voice user experience has some of its own design principles.

Figure 3-22. *Multi-modal conversation across devices*

A big part of this transformation will be long memory. When you come back to a system, it will remember where you left off. Reminding us of what we were working on and what we need to get done. In Figure 3-23, the agent remembers the previous conversation and provides relevant information to the user.

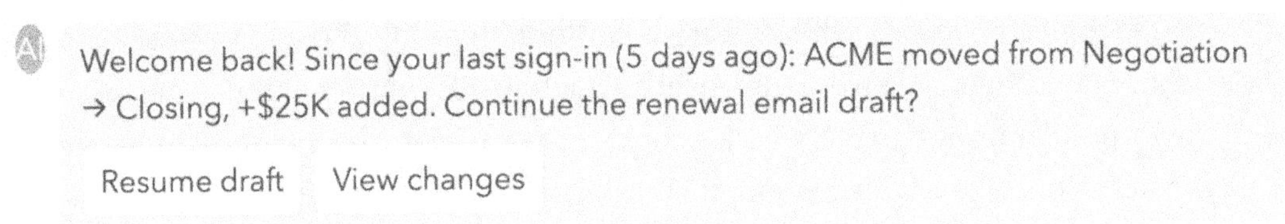

Figure 3-23. *Long memory welcoming user back with updates*

Summary

When people think of the history of computers, everyone has some computer in mind. For me, it is the colorful iMacs from the 1990s. I remember the first time I saw those iMacs, I realized computers were going to be more than just something for geeks like me.

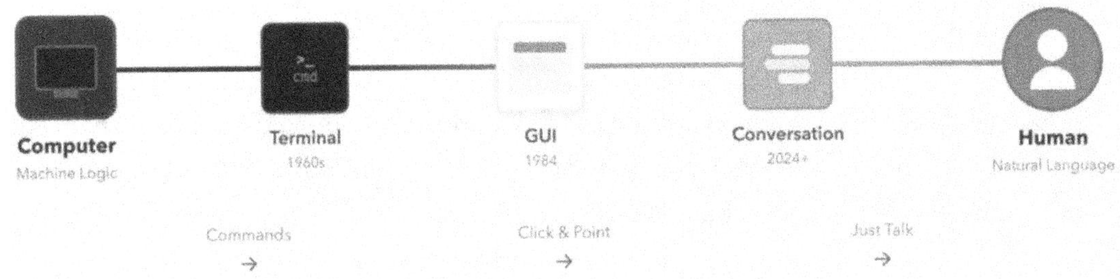

Figure 3-24. *Brief history of user interfaces*

However, the history of software is marked by the history of user interfaces. Many of us grew up on the bland DOS terminals of the 1980s, or maybe the green screens of Apple II. But with each new round of technology, our interfaces changed and evolved, but they were still largely focused on making us operate more like computers.

We were bridging the gap because the machine couldn't, so we went the last mile. Computers couldn't understand us, but we can understand forms, controls, and buttons. But with the advent of LLMs, the gap moved. Computers could interact with us, like us, in a conversation. This shifts the last mile from us interacting like computers can understand, to computers interacting as we can understand. The profoundness of this shift is why everyone finds LLMs so appealing. Figure 3-24 shows a brief overview of the history of user interfaces.

Many will argue that people's conversations aren't that great an interface for computers. And conversations are most certainly not the only useful interface. In many circumstances, traditional forms, controls, and buttons will be better. But some of the most technically demanding users have turned to conversations as their primary mode of computer interaction. These users are developers. And developers are already interacting with an AI Agent as their primary way to create software programs. It is only a matter of time before other engineering disciplines pick up this pattern. And only a matter of time before your grandma is chatting with her computer. Figure 3-25 shows a user experience, focused on an agent chat.

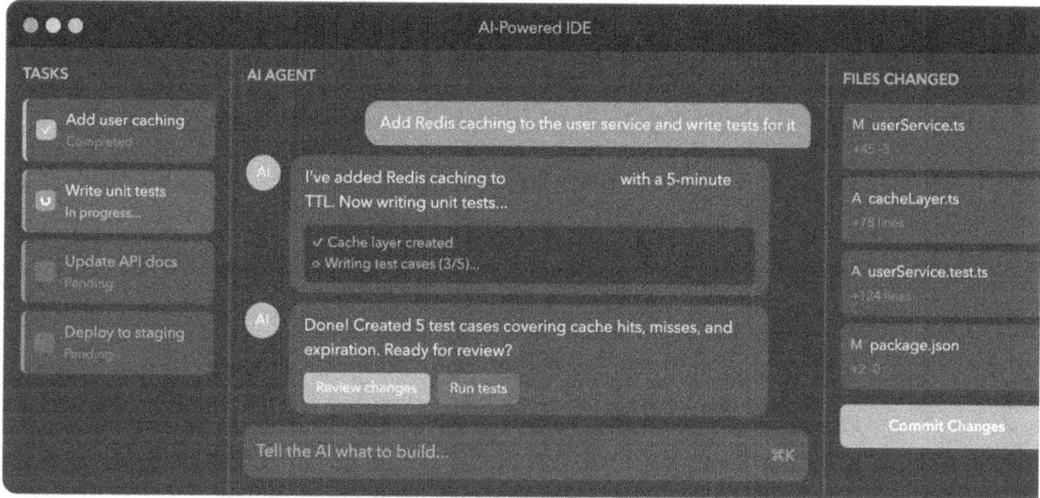

Figure 3-25. *Agentic-based user experience*

LLMs are not the only technical advancement enabling this revolution in user experience. This revolution requires many advancements working together to create conversational experiences that can rival existing solutions. In Chapter 4, we will look at those technical advances.

Key Takeaways

- Conversational interfaces finally make things feel natural. Say what you want and it usually gets it.

- LLMs change the game. All of the old attempts at natural language interfaces fell flat because they were brittle decision trees wanting to be smart. Now, we actually have something that can respond with dynamic text based on user-inputted text.

- The classic UX principles still matter. They just show up differently. Usability, accessibility, clear affordances, consistency, and good error handling still matter. They just need to be rethought for conversational experiences.

- Buttons and forms aren't dead. They're still the right tool for structured data, especially when validation is required.

- You have to design for everyone at once; novice, developers, and power users want different types of interactions, but a good conversations system should be able to serve all three.

- Multi-modal user experiences are coming fast. Voice, text, and visuals all mixed together. The winners will be systems that can adapt gracefully to the desires of the users.

CHAPTER 4

Technical Innovations

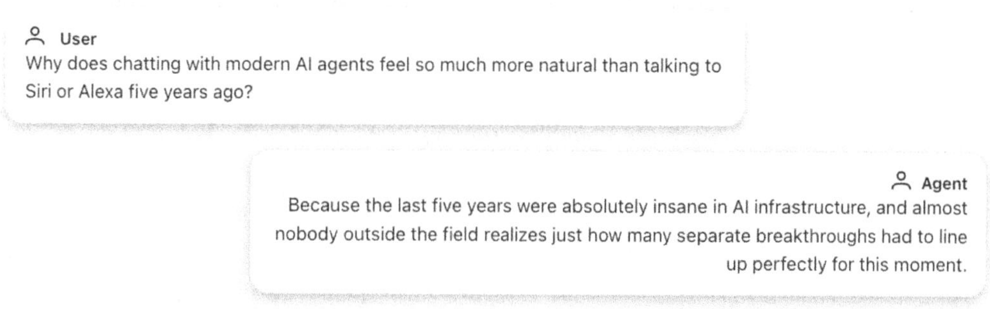

Figure 4-1. *Technical innovations enabling conversational UX*

In this chapter, we discuss many of the leaps that are enabling us to create a better chat experience for our users.

Brief History

Computers exist for humans, which requires them to have ways for humans to issue commands or queries. For years, this was in the form of CLIs (Command-Line Interfaces). In the 1980s, we started the move to GUIs (Graphical User Interfaces). And the next revolution is conversational experiences as shown in Figure 4-1.

In traditional UX, we have forms that users interact with to achieve their goals. These forms often have fields (with data) or buttons to take actions (such as Save). Through this paradigm, we have built many different form types.

A common form type in a traditional form UX is a data table that shows a list of our contacts. We would use some form like this to narrow in on a single contact (Figure 4-2).

C. Michel, *From Buttons to Conversations*, https://doi.org/10.1007/979-8-8688-2688-7_4

EXAMPLE CONTACT TABLE

Name	Email	Company	Tags
Rachel Kim	rachel@acmecorp.com	Acme Corp	VP, Procurement
John Smith	john@techstart.io	TechStart	CTO, Enterprise
Sarah Johnson	sarah@designco.com	Design Co	Creative Director
Mike Chen	mike@financeplus.net	Finance Plus	CEO, Renewals

Figure 4-2. *Traditional data table interface for user search*

Once we find our single user, we would navigate to a new form, often with some editable fields. You can see a form for creating a contact below. Users enter very specific name, email, company, and phone number fields.

Another very common form paradigm is a report into the data, for example, users might want to see contacts by state. We would navigate to a page within the system that displays contacts by state (Figure 4-3). We would often have a separate page to show contact by different dimensions such as sales rep.

Contacts by State

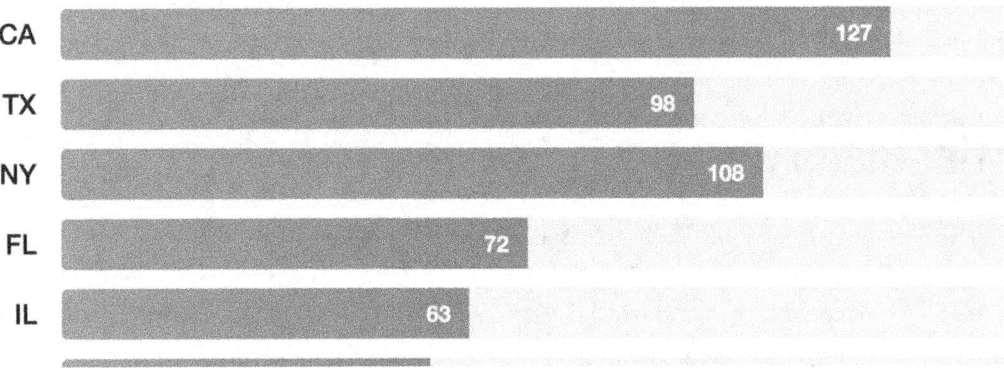

Figure 4-3. *Standard reporting interface showing data visualization*

How does this play out with real work scenarios? Let's assume we want to find out who the primary contact is at Acme regarding renewals. In a traditional UX experience, we would first navigate to a search/table to find an Acme contact (Figure 4-4).

acme

Company Name	Industry	Location	Contacts
Acme Corp	Technology	San Francisco, CA	3 contacts
Acme Industries	Manufacturing	Detroit, MI	1 contact
Acme Solutions	Consulting	Austin, TX	2 contacts

Figure 4-4. *Traditional search workflow to find member information*

After finding the member, we will navigate to a page showing us the member information. On that page, we will find the primary contact and get our answer. In Figure 4-5, you can see a contact form with a field for Primary Contact.

COMPANY INFORMATION

Company Name *

Acme Corp

Industry

Technology

Location

San Francisco, CA

Website

https://acmecorp.com

Primary Contact *

Rachel Kim (VP Procurement) ⌄

Figure 4-5. *Member details form in traditional UX*

Conversational UX can turn this on its head, where instead of navigating through a series of tables and forms, a user can ask their question. Figure 4-6 shows a similar search for a primary contact. Searching for a contact is a simple question.

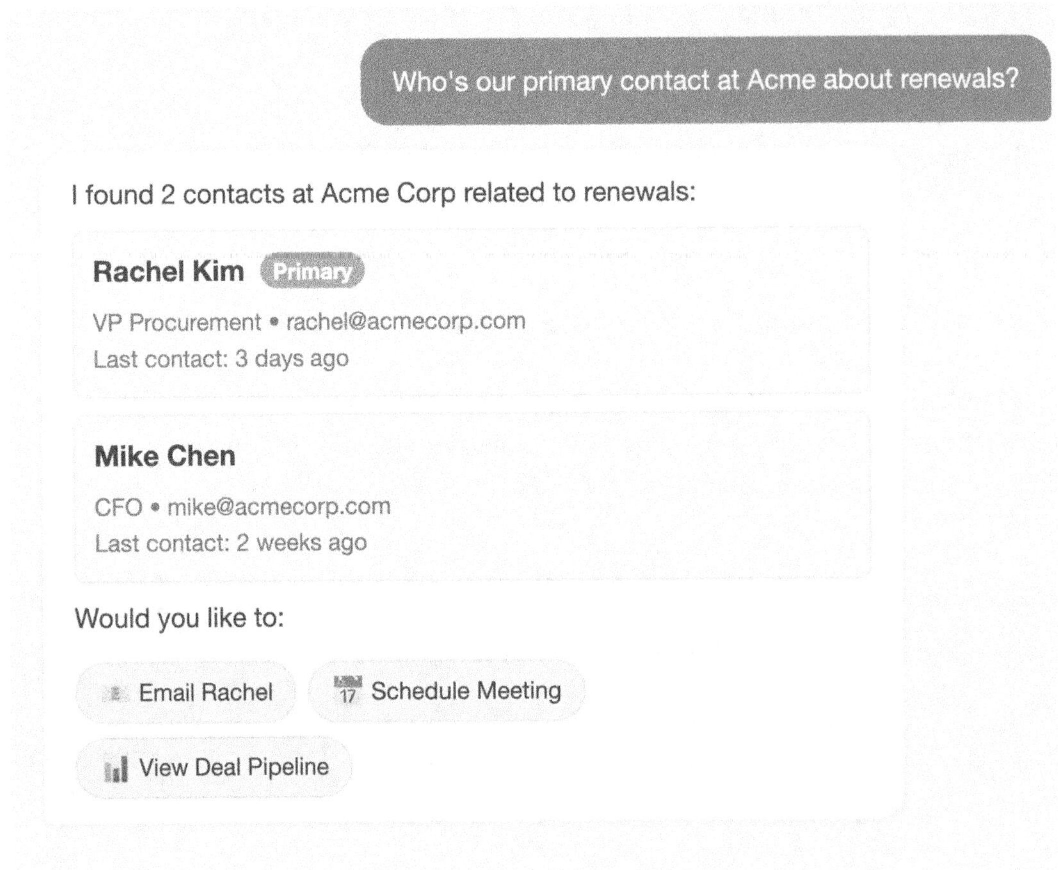

Figure 4-6. *Conversational interface for member lookup*

We can continue to have context-based conversations. Asking a simple "Show me Rachel's recent interactions" would know which Rachel because of the context of the current conversation (Figure 4-7). This ability to retain context and continue the conversation deeper is a huge advantage for conversational systems. Because we have the context of contact, we can use that to provide likely recommended next actions for the user.

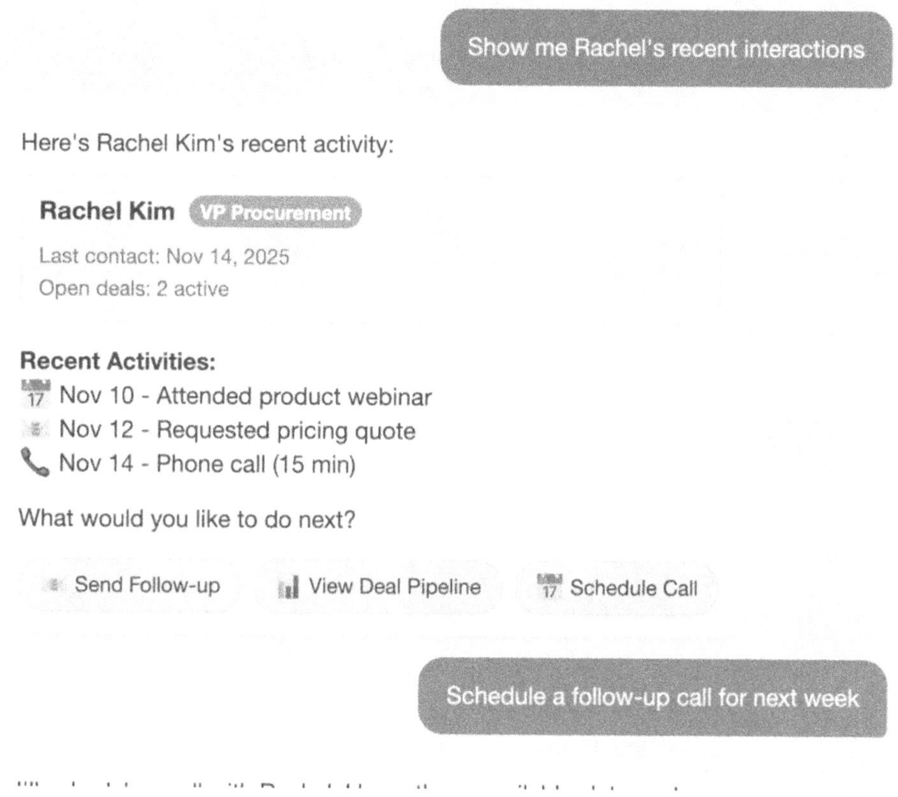

Figure 4-7. *Context-based conversation with follow-up questions*

Even our reporting example from before could be reimagined as a conversation. Instead of finding a "Contacts by State" report, we could ask for contact counts by state. The agent could respond with data, and potentially in a bar chart like form too (Figure 4-8). Building reports probably seems like a stretch, but think of the ultra-complex report builder interfaces users suffer through today.

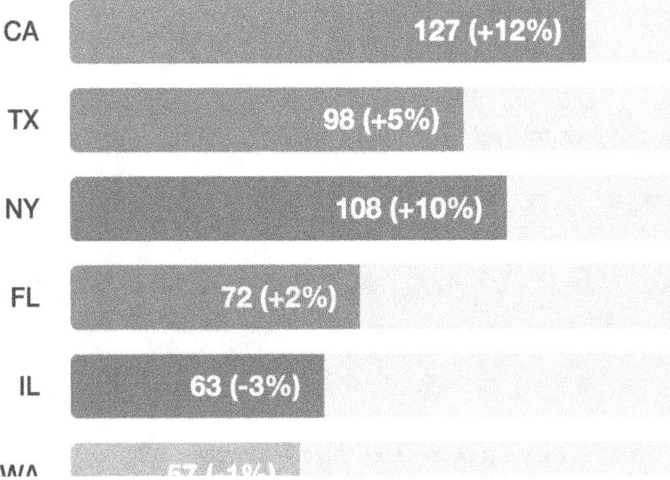

Figure 4-8. *Conversational approach to report generation*

Conversations are not just useful for retrieving information or answering questions. They can be used to update data too. A common use case in software is the uploading of a CSV (comma-separated value) file. In most software, there is an upload button somewhere within the software. Users click this button, then try to upload a file that matches a predetermined CSV format.

This approach sort of works. This approach often has a discoverability problem; users don't know where to go to achieve this. The second problem with this approach, and often a bigger problem, is that users have a difficult time getting data into a known format. An AI conversation agent is better suited to help with both of these problems.

With a conversation, we can ask for a file to be uploaded. The system can interrogate the file to determine the type of data, and the mapping of the data to existing known columns in our database. Imagine a world where you just move your data into a new system with a file upload, without first having to format the data (Figure 4-9).

conference_leads.csv uploaded
142 rows • 8 columns • 24 KB

I've analyzed your CSV file. Here's what I found:

Detected Columns:
- First Name, Last Name → Name
- Email Address → Email
- Company Name → Company
- Job Title → Title
- Phone, State, Industry → Matched

! Issues Found:
- 8 rows missing email addresses
- 3 potential duplicates (same email)
- 12 phone numbers need formatting

I can auto-fix the phone formatting and flag duplicates. Should I proceed with import?

Import (134 valid)   Review Issues   Adjust Mapping

Figure 4-9. *File upload through conversational interface*

Each type of user experience option has advantages and disadvantages. The table below enumerates some of the advantages and disadvantages of using conversations vs. traditional forms. A key insight would be that the best UX going forward will be a blend of both conversational UX and traditional forms.

Aspect	Traditional Forms	Conversational
Learning Curve	Must learn interface and field meanings	Natural language, minimal training
Flexibility	Requires complete, structured input	Handles ambiguity and partial info
Efficiency – Simple	Fast direct access	Slower for single field updates
Efficiency – Complex	Requires navigation	Faster for multi-step workflows
Discoverability	All fields/options displayed upfront	Features not immediately visible

(continued)

Aspect	Traditional Forms	Conversational
Accessibility	Requires precise input	Voice, natural language, low precision input
Cost/Performance	Predictable, minimal compute	Variables
Power Users	Tab navigation, keyboard shortcuts	Verbose for repetitive tasks

If conversational UX is so amazing, why haven't we been doing it? We have just poorly. I worked on a project a few years ago that simulated a conversational experience, but was just a big nested menu. You can see this in the example below. Users can select many options, but they have to stay within those options (Figure 4-10).

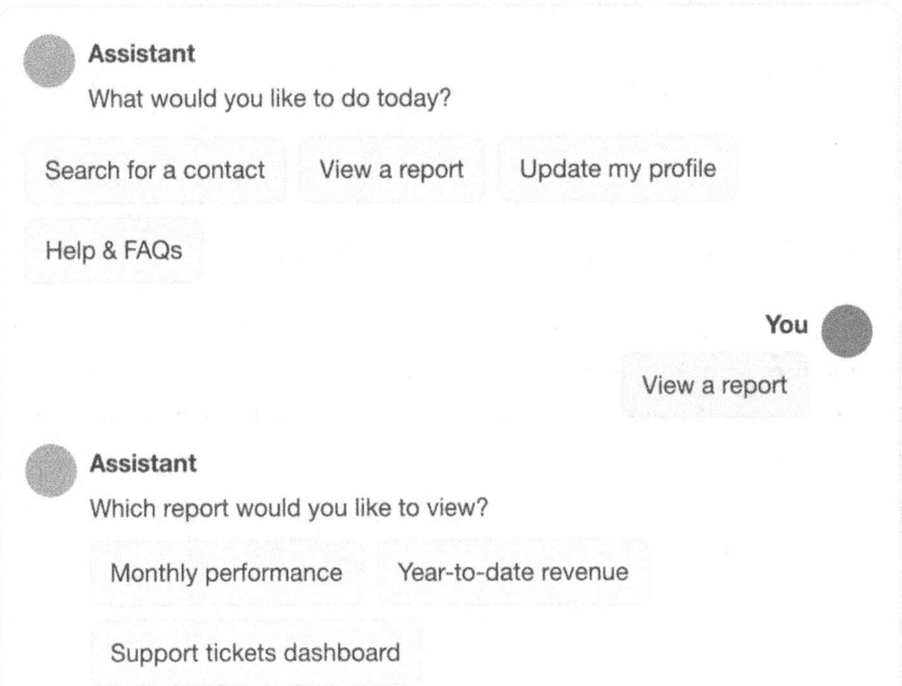

Figure 4-10. *Traditional form vs. conversational UX comparison*

But because of a few technological leaps, we can now allow users to interact by purely typing (or even saying) what they want.

These leaps are

- Model Scale and the Birth of Useful LLMs

- Retrieval-Augmented Generation (RAG)

- MCP (Model Context Protocol)—Enabling models to perform actions

- Dialog Management Moves from Rules to Agents

- Streaming, Latency Tricks, and the "Instant Response" Illusion

Leap 1: Model Scale and the Birth of Useful LLMs

LLMs seem miraculous, but when I first started using them, they felt more like auto-complete on steroids. In the early days, we were using LLMs to complete small amounts of code, which wasn't that much different than the auto-complete feature of many IDEs.

My software development began before auto-complete was a thing. During this period, we had to remember the names of methods/functions. We had to remember the order of the parameters.

During the late 1990s, development IDEs started to help us fill in the method names and the parameters. We no longer had to remember as much, and when we compiled our programs, the likelihood that everything would be built the first time went up a lot. This was a big enhancement for our productivity, and let us focus on writing code and solving problems, and not memorization. And as someone with a bad memory, not having to use it as much was a big boon for me.

In the early 2000s, these features in IDEs exploded, which was a big reason why TypeScript was created. TypeScript is effectively a pre-compiler on top of JavaScript. JavaScript is a dynamic programming language, but being fully dynamic it is hard to implement auto-complete. For auto-complete to work, it is a lot easier if the method names are known. But with a fully dynamic language, those things can only be determined at runtime. Hence, the real advantage of TypeScript over JavaScript is that auto-complete could be built.

The amazing thing about LLMs they can provide an excellent auto-complete, and a much larger auto-complete without requiring those type hints. LLMs do not require us to build the syntax of our languages rigidly for the LLM to predict the next word.

And LLMs have another big advantage, they can guess more than just the next word. They can take the name of a method and predict the entire content of the method or function.

A big part of this advantage isn't just that LLMs can do this, but that they can do it quickly. If it took hours to get the auto-complete, it wouldn't be useful, but LLMs are fast. Often, implementing an entire function or method takes less than a second.

Another way of thinking about this is the "Improv Actor Analogy." With this analogy, we have an actor who has read every script ever written. When asked to do an improv scene, the actor would synthesize their knowledge of existing scripts to determine how the actor should respond. Since the actor has full access to all scripts (LLMs are training on massive amounts of data), he can quickly respond with words, dialog, and actions that fit the improv scene.

LLMs are essentially giant neural networks training to master next-word prediction, which is why the improv actor analogy is so fitting. At LLMs' core, they're made up of billions of interconnected parameters organized into layers of artificial neurons. These neurons are trained on enormous amounts of text, and during the training the network learns to adjust its weights so it can spot subtle statistical patterns in how words, ideas, and concepts flow together.

Once the neural network is trained, it doesn't actually know anything. You give it a prompt, it breaks the text into tokens, turns them into numerical embeddings, and then the neural network calculates probabilities for what should come next. It predicts one token at a time, adds it back in, and keeps going until the response is complete. The magic comes from the scale of these neural networks.

LLMs are the heart of this AI agent/conversation revolution that is occurring in user experience. Without fast text-based responses, we would be really hampered with what we can do, but luckily, we have LLMs. And when we pair LLMs with some of the other leaps in the next section, we can create some powerful conversational experiences. LLMs enable the conversational user experiences we have long desired.

Leap 2: Retrieval-Augmented Generation (RAG)

LLMs are amazing at answering questions where the answer is within general knowledge. But they are unable to answer questions for data they don't have access to. An LLM can't answer the question, who is the primary contact for Acme Corp. These queries often require access to our private data.

Sometimes it isn't access to private data, it can just be domain-specific data. LLMs are trained on a lot, but what if the question is domain-specific. A good example here would be using a company blog to answer questions. The company's blog is probably public, but also probably not part of the training data.

Also, if we want to make LLMs useful, we have to address the hallucination problem. LLMs are amazing because they can answer almost any question, but that also comes at the cost that they will often make up information or hallucinate answers. LLMs' tendency to hallucinate results is well-documented and a core concern in using them. But with RAG our LLMs can create responses grounded in real data. This grounding in real data allows us to trust the responses. And by providing clear citations, users can verify the results. We could solve these problems by training models on our private or domain-specific data. That solution is available, but it can be expensive, especially if we want to retrain frequently. These types of problems are a good example where Retrieval-Augmented Generation (RAG) is a great option.

With RAG, we search a vector database to find results matching the user's query. Then we take those results plus the question and send them to an LLM to generate a response.

RAG has three phases:

- **Retrieval:** Query a vector database. Retrieve documents.

- **Augmentation:** Combine retrieved results with query.

- **Generation:** Use LLM to generate a response.

As an example, we could ask, "Summarize recent interactions with Rachel before I call her." With a question like this, we would first find relevant interactions by using a vector database search. Then we would load those interactions. Then we would send those documents, the original question, to an LLM to answer the question. A potential example of this is shown in Figure 4-11.

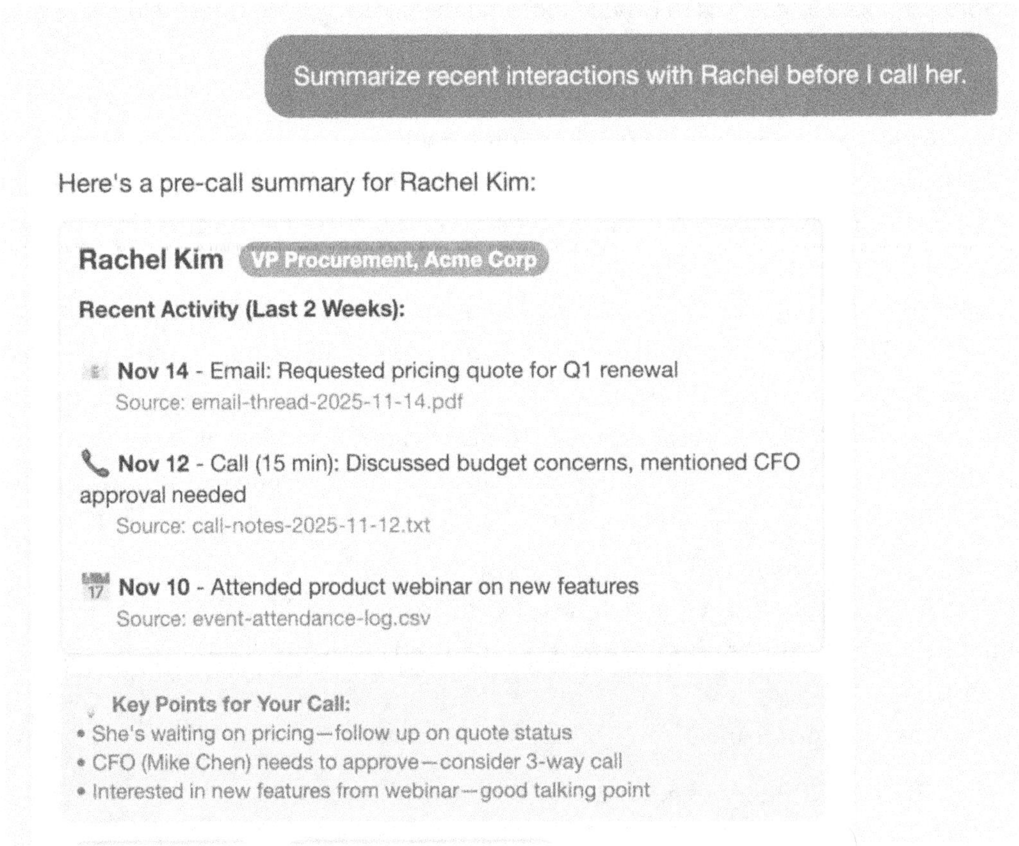

Figure 4-11. *Vector-embedding process for RAG*

Another example could be asking questions about blog content. Let's assume we want to ask, "Can you find me an article about how to build a RAG?" With this question, we would first do a vector search to find relevant blog content. Then we would load those blog posts. We would send those blog posts and the original question to an LLM, and the LLM would generate a response. Figure 4-12 is a sample result of this query from my website. I asked the question, "Can you find me an article about how to build a RAG?"

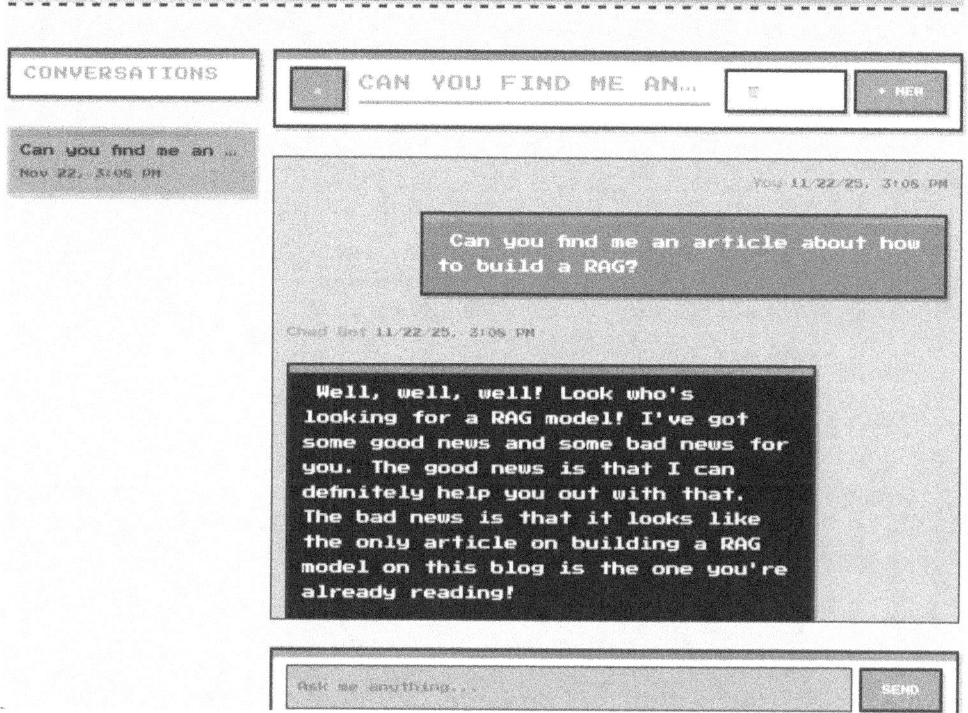

Figure 4-12. *RAG retrieval process: Query to relevant documents*

There are a lot of things going on to make this happen. The diagram shows the query processing flow in an RAG system. The user asks a question. The system converts the question into a question vector. The question vector is used to search for similarity in the vector database. The results from that search are sent to the retriever to load the documents. The documents, the question, and the context are sent to the LLM to generate an answer. Figure 4-13 shows a sequence diagram denoting the process for retrieving documents.

Query Processing Flow

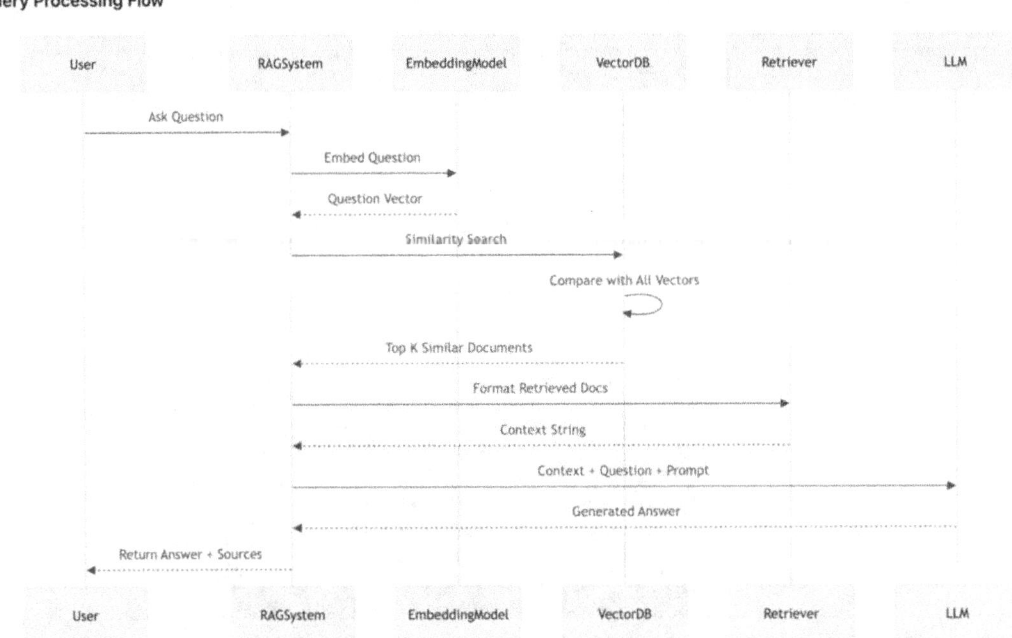

Figure 4-13. *RAG augmentation: Combining retrieved context with query*

RAG has quickly become a standard for retrieving information for use by an LLM. Building RAG solutions is easy to do, but there is already a plethora of pre-made services that will handle this complexity for you. Figure 4-14 shows how RAG is used to answer a question.

RAG isn't a solution for all problems, especially if we need to update data. In the next section, we will look into a solution to that problem.

Leap 3: MCP (Model Context Protocol)

RAG provides a great option for enabling AI to appear to have access to our data, but for AI (LLMs) to really achieve goals for us, they will need a way to change data. Model Context Protocol (MCP) provides a way for AI agents to interact with our systems.

LLMs are basically big text completion machines, they have no ability to reach out and access data, or to reach out and change data. MCP could be seen as the USB for LLMs. USB is a universal connector that allows our computers to communicate with other devices. Sometimes with USB, our computers send information to other devices, sometimes our devices pull information from other devices, and sometimes it is both.

MCP isn't completely novel, and with a functional calling approach, we can solve the same problems. But with MCP, we have a standard protocol that can be reused. USB is not the best protocol for all forms of communication, but because it is a well-known protocol with a port on every computer, it is the go-to for communication. MCP is becoming a common protocol for AI agents, enabling them to communicate with other systems.

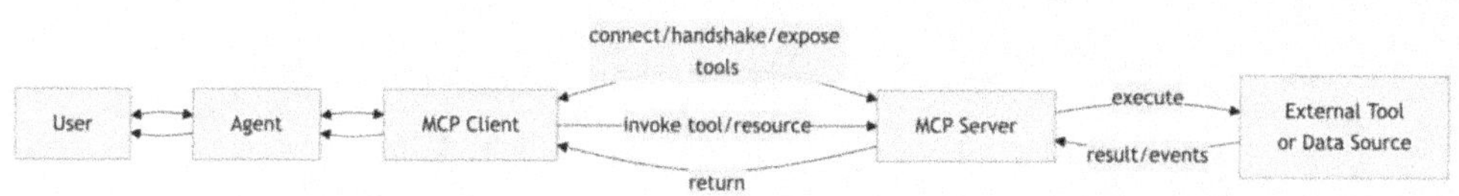

Figure 4-14.   Complete RAG pipeline flow

With MCP, our AI agent can do things like sending an email. In Figure 4-15, we ask for all unpaid invoices. Then the user clicks "Send" next to the "Bob Smith" invoice. The query to get all unpaid invoices could be a query tool call to an MCP server. When the user clicks send and sends a notice to Bob, that could also call an MCP tool to send a notification.

Invoice	Customer	Amount · Due	Action
INV-1041	Amanda Lee	$1,280 • 12/05	Send
INV-1042	Bob Smith	$2,450 • 12/10	Send
INV-1043	Central Logistics	$980 • 12/12	Send

Figure 4-15.   MCP architecture: model interacting with external tools

From a conversation perspective, we could use MCP and RAG in the same request. User asks, "What's the status of our deal with Acme Corp, and remind me what we discussed in our last call?" The AI agent could use the MCP to look up the status of the deal with Acme Corp., and use RAG to retrieve the notes from the last call with Acme Corp (Figure 4-16).

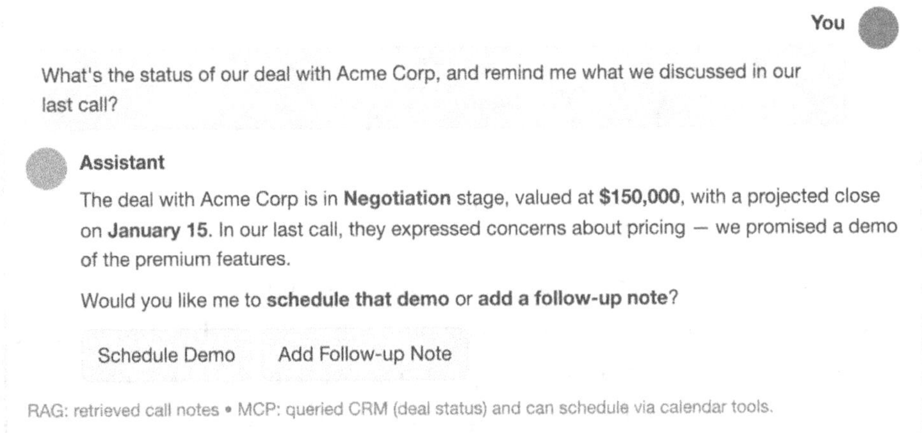

Figure 4-16. *MCP tools enabling system integrations*

MCP is still very new, but it is already being used by everyone who wants to expose their systems to AI agents. MCP is already the USB for AI agents, with many major sites supporting a form of MCP interaction today.

Leap 4: Dialog Management

As we move into the world of AI agent-driven dialog management, we will encounter new technical challenges. These technical challenges seem small, but they are crucial to creating a solid conversational experience.

First among these challenges is state tracking, which involves remembering the conversation context. This challenge has many issues, first is the natural ambiguities in languages, and the fact that conversations shift over time. Also, LLMs have a max number of tokens available; we can't just keep sending the entire conversation back with each new message.

Another problem is handling the dynamic flows that occur with user conversations. Users change topics frequently, with new goals. Handling these transitions will be particularly difficult.

The ability for conversations to call tools, and when to call which tool is a challenge. While many tools (RAG/MCP) are emerging, the overall pattern and process for interacting with these is still evolving.

Error handling is difficult in a non-structured world. And when users get into a bad state, resetting into a good state. These are non-trivial problems, and if we look at our ability to handle errors on websites, our ability to handle errors in these situations should concern us.

Another issue to work through is setting good guardrails around the conversations. If we are building an agent chat experience for our CRM, we probably don't want to enable users to ask questions about their favorite movie star. We will want the chat to be limited to our CRM.

There is already a lot of literature out there on how to handle these conversations. But the diagram in Figure 4-17 will appear very similar to other solutions. Users submit a message. The agent receives the message. The system uses NLU (Natural Language Understanding) to figure out the intent. The dialog state tracker is updated with the intent. From there, Dialog Policy takes over, and determines how to route the request. If we can, we will respond immediately. If we can't respond immediately or if we need to ask for more information, we will push onto the NLG (Natural Language Generation) to form a response to the user. If we need to use a tool to complete the quest for the user, we will send the request to the tool. Then feed the response of the tool back to the dialog state management and start the decision process over.

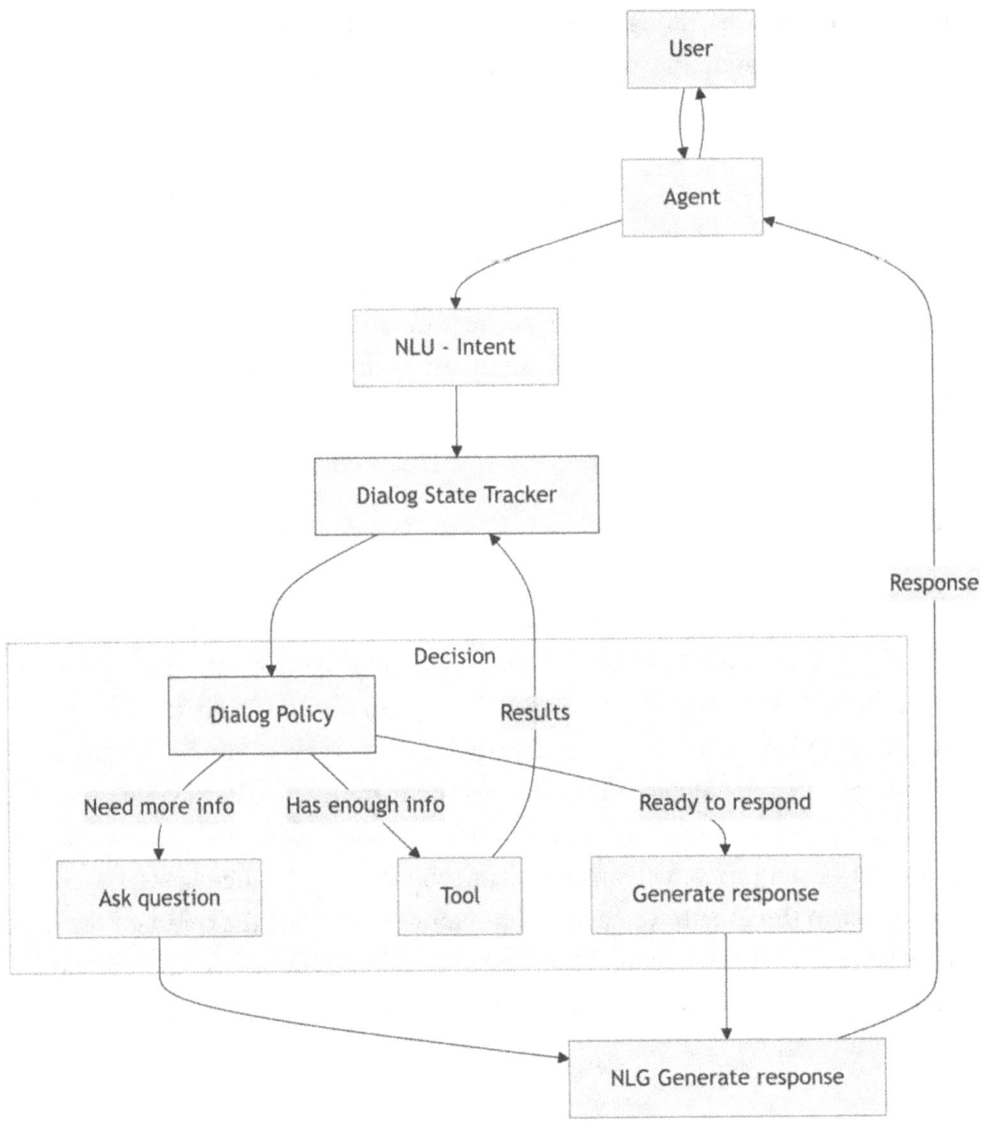

Figure 4-17. *Dialog state management in conversational systems*

The good news is that this problem of Dialog Management or Conversation Management is a well-known problem with many people working to solve it. The big cloud providers already have solution to handle most of these problems for you. And in reality, this is probably the best option to handle these for your solution. There are open source solutions to these problems, too.

Leap 5: "Instant Response" Illusion

It is amazing how much software is really being implemented in some sort of spreadsheet (like Microsoft Excel). The number of internal applications that should exist but don't, or never get fully pulled out of spreadsheets, is kind of amazing. Part of the reason is that people understand spreadsheets. But another part of that reason is that spreadsheets are fast with almost no latency. You don't have to reload a form every time we want to make a change. We just made the change.

Latency matters a lot in UX, it especially matters if actions are perceived as slow. If user experience is perceived as slow, users will quickly give up on using your application or try a different way to solve the problem. And this is where LLMs, tools (MCP/RAG), pose a problem for us. While they are faster and getting faster. They are not as fast as making a basic web call to a backend. A web call can be relatively fast, less than half a second. But most calls to LLMs are going to take over a second, potentially multiple.

Component	Latency
Web API Call	0.5 seconds (or less)
LLM Only	1 to 3 seconds
LLM using Tools	2 to 6 seconds
Complex agent workflows	8 to 20 seconds

LLMs are inherently slower than the Web API calls we have built our applications on. Actually, using tools (MCP/RAG) is going to typically add a Web API Call time to an existing slow process.

Slower processes and slower responses for our users are not what they want; they want their results, and they want them now.

Solving this problem is twofold. The first and obvious is making LLMs faster, their responses faster. Also, anything we can do to make the tools consumed faster will help in this too. The second part of this solution is token streaming. With token streaming, we do not wait for all tokens to be returned to show the results in the user interface; we start streaming that as soon as they are available.

With token streaming, we do not reduce the overall time to answer a question. But instead, we reduce the amount of time our agents take to start responding to users.

In the example in Figure 4-18, the user is stalled on the response until the entire response is available.

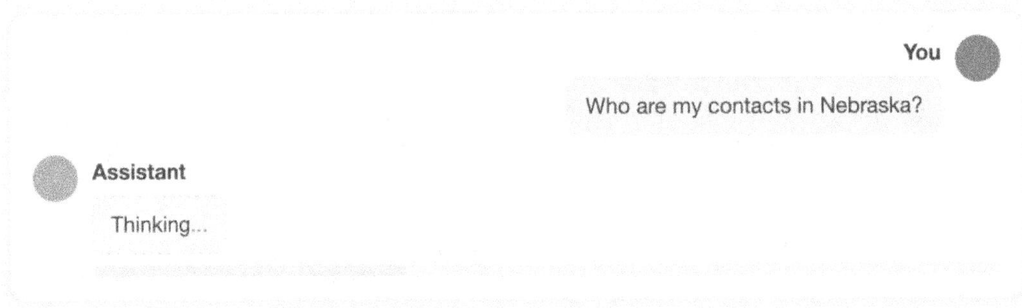

Figure 4-18. *Agent-based dialog management architecture*

In this second example, we are streaming contacts as soon as we start to receive them from the LLM (Figure 4-19).

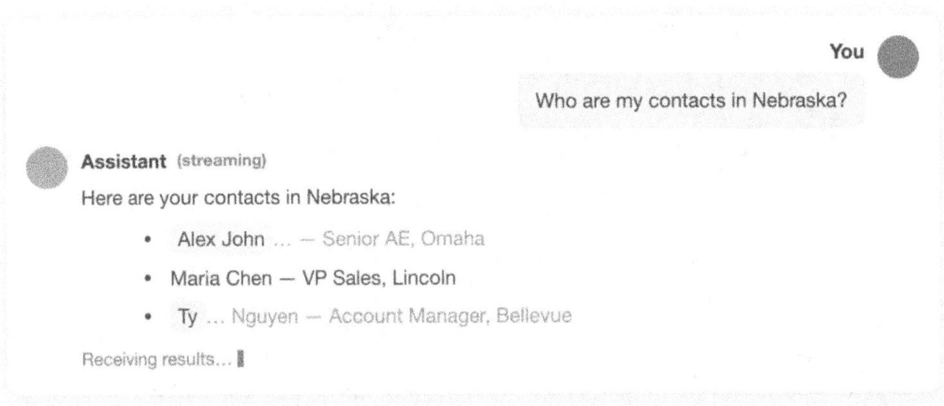

Figure 4-19. *Streaming response with progressive rendering*

Token streaming is not a solution for all performance issues we will have with our AI conversations, but it can help reduce the perception of slowness.

Summary

Did we change the UI, or did we give the machine a mind and a memory? LLMs without the ability to interact with us in a conversational format would be limiting, but interacting in a conversational way has many challenges. Each of these challenges can be solved, and in this chapter, we discussed many of the leaps that are enabling us to create a better chat experience for our users. We have not discussed every leap, but the ones that lend themselves the most to enabling great chat experiences.

Many of these leaps will be handled for you by your selection of an online platform to help you implement chat within your application. The likelihood that you have to implement RAG is pretty low; there are a lot of great options out there already. But, knowing these issues and being aware can help us build better experiences, and make better choices in technology.

Key Takeaways

- LLMs are the engine behind conversational user experience.

- RAG enables conversations to have access to internal information and provide citations to build trust.

- MCP turns conversations into workflows by allowing the conversations to communicate with external systems.

- Dialog management is a required skill in this age of conversational experiences.

- Perceived speed matters a lot to enable conversational experiences.

Bibliography

Chen, M., et al. (2024). Metron: Holistic performance evaluation framework for LLM inference systems. arXiv preprint arXiv:2407.07000. https://arxiv.org/abs/2407.07000(Provides detailed benchmarks for TTFT, output speed, and tool-use overhead across providers.)

Hoffmann, J., Borgeaud, S., Mensch, A., Buchatskaya, E., Cai, T., Rutherford, E., de Las Casas, D., Hendricks, L. A., Welbl, J., Clark, A., Hennigan, T., Noland, E., Millican, K., van den Driessche, G., Damoc, B., Guy, A., Osindero, S., Simonyan, K., Elsen, E., Rae, J. W., Vinyals, O., and Sifre, L. (2022). Training compute-optimal large language models. arXiv preprint arXiv:2203.15556. https://arxiv.org/abs/2203.15556

Kaplan, J., McCandlish, S., Henighan, T., Brown, T. B., Chess, B., Child, R., Gray, S., Radford, A., Wu, J., and Amodei, D. (2020). Scaling laws for neural language models. arXiv preprint arXiv:2001.08361. https://arxiv.org/abs/2001.08361

Patrick Lewis, Ethan Perez, Aleksandra Piktus, Fabio Petroni, Vladimir Karpukhin, Naman Goyal, Heinrich Küttler, Mike Lewis, Wen-tau Yih, Tim Rocktäschel, Sebastian Riedel, and Douwe Kiela. (2020). "Retrieval-Augmented Generation for Knowledge-Intensive NLP Tasks." Advances in Neural Information Processing Systems (NeurIPS) 33. https://arxiv.org/abs/2005.11401

Young, S., Gašić, M., Thomson, B., and Williams, J. D. (2013). POMDP-based statistical spoken dialog systems: A review. Proceedings of the IEEE, 101(5), 1160–1179. https://doi.org/10.1109/JPROC.2012.2225812

CHAPTER 5

Integrating Conversations into Existing Applications

User
Help me refactor this 400-line monster function? It's scaring my coworkers.AI:
4000 lines?

AI
Bold of you to call that a 'function' instead of a crime scene.

Figure 5-1. *This figure is a conversation between a user and an AI Agent. The User is asking for help refactoring a function with 4000 lines, and the AI makes a joke about that not being a function, but a crime scene*

Most work is done on large existing systems. This chapter will provide strategies for extending conversations into those systems.

The majority of the time developers spend is in existing codebases. And most users interact with systems that were not made in the last year. They probably had development in the last year, but the majority of the work on the platform was in the past.

That isn't a problem, it is just a fact that the majority of software, and the majority of the work on software, occurs in existing code bases. These existing code bases drive the majority of software use today.

These existing code bases are often older than you might imagine. It is not uncommon for these systems to have code bases that have been under development for 10 years. A 10-year-old system will have some technical debt. See Figure 5-1 for a joke about a 4000-line function being a crime scene.

Technical debt is the difference between a clean/ideally maintainable system and the version implemented. Technical debt can be very difficult to quantify because the ideal version of software is not obvious. And if we can't easily determine the ideal version, how can we determine how far off from the ideal we are?

Sometimes people will describe technical debt as a mortgage we have to pay on. Since we have a mortgage, we have to pay on that debt. Paying on that debt reduces the amount of money we have available. If we didn't have that mortgage, we would have more money to spend on other things. With technical debt, because we are carrying that debt, we will not be able to move as fast.

While this isn't a book on technical debt, I do think it is important to realize that the older systems carry some debt that can make big changes difficult. This might make us want to think that, with this level of change (adding conversations), we should just do an entire rewrite.

Rewrites are almost always the wrong solution. There are counterexamples, but more often than not, rewrites end up failing. The reasons rewrites fail are complex, but here is a quick list:

- The existing system is almost always more complex than assumed.

- Work will continue on the existing system, making it difficult to catch up.

- This will require splitting the team into "new" team and "maintenance" team, effectively limiting the velocity of both.

I will be honest that I feel the primary reason developers want to do rewrites is that it sounds like more fun and easier. Both of which are probably lies the developers are telling themselves. It might be more fun for a while, but as the pressure to deliver comes, it will result in an emotion rollercoaster that is most certainly not fun. And building from scratch will lose all of the existing bug fixes. When someone says, "let's do the rewrite," the right answer is almost always "no."

With this push to conversations, or AI-first, there will be a big push to rewrite, and many will push for that massive rewrite. That will almost certainly be a failure for any reasonably large system.

Challenges

Changing any system is difficult, and making fundamental changes to any system is very difficult. Anyone who has experienced changing any existing software system knows this to be true. These systems are often branded as legacy or brownfield. These legacy systems carry with them a legacy of software that can be challenging. This difficulty is multifold.

Trying to update these systems has many technical challenges. First, legacy systems are often built on older technologies. These technologies are often more difficult to use with modern technologies and patterns. Second, data formats change over time, and integrating new and legacy systems can pose data challenges. Another common challenge with legacy systems is that the authentication can be antiquated and difficult to integrate with newer systems.

While technical challenges can be problematic, there are often bigger sorts of problems. Organizational or people problems are often harder to address.

There can be many types of organizational problems with change. The first is getting everyone aligned. Often, achieving a big change can require working with many teams with different leadership. This can be an almost impassable problem.

Another organizational problem can be risk aversion. People are often opposed to any big change. People tend to like the certainty of the risk of something better. This desire for certainty can stifle innovation within an organization.

The biggest reason things don't change is budget and timeline pressures. Developers are often under pressure to achieve the next big feature, and the added pressure of adding a new technology or new approach will seem like too big a risk to take.

All of these risks are real. People have good reason to be worried about big changes in any system. Below, I present five rules for adding conversational experiences

Five Rules of Adding AI

There are no absolute rules for being successful with AI, but here are five rules for adding AI to your legacy system. These rules will help you achieve a migration to an AI-first system.

These rules do have an order, but you should probably do all of them to start your AI journey. Some of these rules will sound like generic legacy migration concepts, but I think the combination of them is what creates a higher likelihood of success.

Start Tiny

Updating legacy systems can be an overwhelming proposition, but like many activities, taking the first step is the most important step. When adding AI to your legacy system, don't bite off too much on the first step.

When leaping AI, a good approach is to start small, and use a read-only approach in our first version. Starting small minimizes the risk and effort. And starting with read-only access to data for the AI agents. Starting with read-only minimizes the security risk and unwanted data updates while helping everyone become comfortable with this new paradigm. In Figure 5-2, an agent is helping a user find data within the system.

A good use would be helping a user find their order. In this situation, we would be providing read-only access, we would get to use context to help queries, and it is a small add with the potential to create a better user experience.

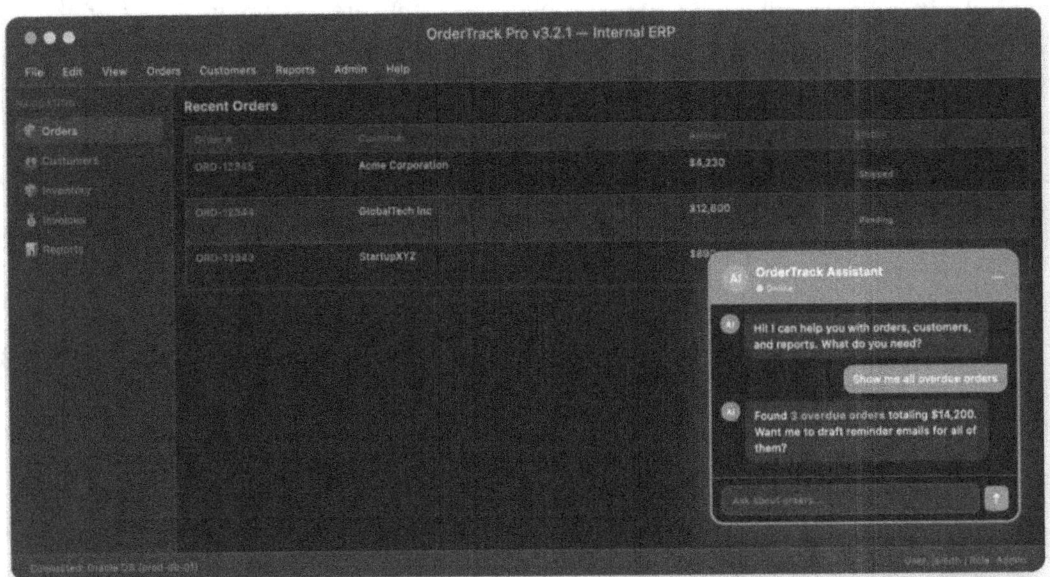

Figure 5-2.   Using an AI assistant to find orders. An assistant is added as a popup over the top of the existing UI

As a litmus test that you have done this correctly, if you turn off the chat tomorrow, the original app should work like before. Hopefully, users will miss the chat application, but they can still complete their work.

Bridge

The next rule applies to pretty much all legacy migrations, which is to use a bridge or facade pattern. With this pattern, we will create a new layer on our system that is a cleaner interface into the system.

Before AI, most legacy migrations used some sort of facade. As an example, the existing legacy API (Application Programming Interface) in the system is probably rough and carries many scars of an API that has existed through many releases. With a legacy migration, we would often want to slowly create a good interface on top of the existing scare-filled API. When adding AI or chat interfaces on top of an existing system, the same rules apply. We will want to create a facade on top of the existing system, and allow our new interface to use our cleaner facade.

If we think about it, adding an AI chat on top of our system is kind of creating a new facade from a user interface perspective. This gives us a newer and simpler interface to our system.

If we were doing a legacy migration of a CRM system, we first choose to build a new facade on top of that system. We would probably pick the area to build the facade based on future features or a desire for a competitive advantage in an area. In this example, let's assume we are building a new facade on top of the event management subsystem. We would create a newer and easier to use API for interacting with events within that system.

If we are adding AI to an existing system, we will follow a similar approach. We will look for an area or subsystem that could benefit from an AI conversational approach. We would then add an AI conversational agent to that subsystem, potentially with only read access to the system.

Lockdown

People will be very concerned about adding AI to their system because of the security risks, and they are correct to be worried. There have been many high-profile examples of security failures involving AI. These concerns are real, and it is best to hit them straight on.

As was mentioned earlier, using read-only calls in your first versions is an effective way to limit potential damage. Another good strategy is to only use existing APIs with your AI agent. Existing APIs will have the correct security permissions in place.

It will be tempting to create a new API for our chat interfaces, and we may eventually need to do so. However, if we can use our existing interfaces, we should. Also, when creating our new chat-based interfaces, we should audit the queries and responses.

As the recommendation in this chapter is useful (read only first), that doesn't stop the leaking of information. We must still obey the rules of our platforms and only allow users to have access to the data they should.

If we are creating new APIs for our AI conversations, we must think through the guardrails as first-class citizens; the security can't be an afterthought.

Add conversations to our systems can be a powerful way to enable our users to get their work done faster, and hence make our products more valuable. But that also means they can create more damage. We must create approval flows for any operation that could affect multiple records. Before conversations changing 100 records in a CRM probably meant opening 100 UI screens and making a change on each one. Now with agents it could be a single request. This is a lot of power, but also a big chance to make big mistakes. We must warn users before allowing them to make any bulk updates in a system.

Pass Context

When you have a conversation with a person, you assume some common starting points, some context. If I am waiting outside to get into a sporting event, I can assume the other people are probably aware of the game. A chat about the state of the team will be appropriate, and I can assume the other person will understand the context.

As we extend our system with AI Agents, we must make those agents understand the context of the software. If our agents are the equivalent of talking to a non-sports fan outside of a sporting event, it is going to be rough.

Without context, AI Chat will often feel like we are talking to someone who isn't in the right place. If we are on an orders screen and asking about our orders, hopefully the AI agent is smart enough to know who the user is and their orders.

Context will make our conversations immediately more useful. Context prevents us from having to tell a big backstory to get the answer we want. And if we are extending our existing system, providing context will enable the conversations to immediately provide more value to the users.

Fallbacks

AI chat will be a scary proposition. The development team will find it scary to add. And the users in many legacy systems will find it concerning. And on top of all of this, legacy systems demand reliability. Legacy systems have many existing users who need to get a task done.

When adding conversations to existing systems, it is tempting to create features that push users to use the new chat feature, or maybe even require the use of the chat. Instead, I recommend always providing a fallback way to solve the problem. We want to augment our legacy system with an AI chat, not replace it.

We will want to build everything into our AI agent chat, but we should be careful to overdo it. Often with these legacy systems, just linking to an existing portion of the system to solve a known problem might be the best option. We shouldn't be afraid to reuse existing components.

While adding AI conversational chat to our legacy systems, it would be easy to add the chat and assume success. We should instrument to see if our conversations are solving real problems for users. Are they getting successful outcomes?

Monkey Ladder Experiment

There is a very famous experiment, and you have maybe heard this before. This experiment is surprising in a couple of ways, but I think there is something we can learn from it.

In this infamous experiment, a group of monkeys is kept in a room. In the room, there is a ladder with bananas at the top. Whenever a monkey climbs the ladder, all the monkeys are sprayed with cold water. The monkeys eventually learn not to climb the ladder.

When a new monkey is introduced, the original monkeys will harshly stop the new monkey from climbing the ladder. Eventually, the original monkeys are replaced one at a time. And each newly introduced monkey learns the lesson that you don't climb the ladder from the other monkeys. After all the original monkeys are gone, and we are left with no monkeys that have ever been sprayed by water, they still won't climb the ladder. This social conditioning is too strong.

This behavior of avoiding the ladder (and the bananas) persisted even after any monkey has ever been sprayed by cold water. The conditioning is so strong that the monkeys avoid going for the bananas.

This story has two lessons for us, both relevant to this situation. First, if any time you want to go for anything, people who have already been burned going for something will try to stop you. This desire to stop you is strong in them; they don't want to get burned (or sprayed with cold water) again. Trying to introduce a conversational experience into our applications will be difficult. People will remember Clippy, or maybe something even worse. But we have to push through to be successful.

Second, the story of the monkey ladder experiment is completely made up. You have probably heard before, and maybe even believed it. The fear of adding an AI chat to our applications is somewhat real, but most of the concerns are made up. People will object for a variety of reasons, but those reasons are things they have just heard. Follow the five steps mentioned above and conquer.

Summary

Legacy systems are complex, usually much more complex than anyone imagines. Moving them to a new paradigm is a challenge from both a technical and an organizational perspective. Having a clear strategy and rules to follow when integrating conversational experiences into existing applications is essential.

Remember the analogy of the monkey ladder experiment. There will be a lot of pressure to keep the status quo, but our systems must evolve. Any change agent in an organization will have many people trying to stop them, but we must continue to push for change.

Key Takeaways

- **Start Tiny:** Think big, but start small.

- **Bridge:** Build the new system in parallel, use the facade pattern to route some traffic to the new implementation.

- **Lockdown:** AI creates new security risks, lockdown security from day one.

- **Pass Context:** Pass as much context as possible. Allow the AI conversations to feel as natural as possible.

- **Fallbacks:** Always have a deterministic fallback. If the new conversation path fails, have a known path to solve the problem.

CHAPTER 6

The Future

Figure 6-1. *This is based on a hilarious AI mishap from 2024. Google's AI Overview feature would suggest mixing about 1/8 cup of non-toxic glue into the sauce. DO NOT PUT GLUE INTO YOUR PIZZA SAUCE*

This chapter looks ahead at the coming wave of AI that's already starting to reshape our user interfaces. The change will be massive, from multi-modal interactions and helpful AI assistants to entirely new AI-first applications. Big shifts are underway. We're standing right at the edge of this wave, and once it hits, nothing is going to look the same again. We have built more and more complex user experiences. This desire for a more complex user experience exists partially because we were constantly trying to build user interfaces that were more usable. In Chapter 2, we discussed many aspects of good user interface design. These principles are still valid today and need to be understood to create good user interfaces. And chat interfaces are not a panacea, we still must create good and relevant information (Figure 6-1 shows the opposite).

We also discussed the three personas: the novice, the Developer, and the Power User. Creating user interfaces that fulfill the desires of each of these users is a big task, and often not practical with one user interface.

C. Michel, *From Buttons to Conversations*, https://doi.org/10.1007/979-8-8688-2688-7_6

In Chapter 3, I discuss the change to a conversational user experience. The wave of this change is going to be big, much bigger than people expect. A conversational user experience doesn't just change one piece of software or one application; most applications will be better off with a conversational experience.

This change is already happening, and we will continue to see its impacts. Developers already operate in a conversational-first mode, and many other roles will be moving conversation-first. Creator-style tasks will often move to a conversational experience.

A conversational experience has many inherent advantages. Humans learn to communicate through conversation at a young age. And we already have a lot of experience communicating through our native languages. But why then haven't we been using them?

We have chosen to use forms and buttons because these structured inputs are easier for computers to process. Support for full natural language text has been a dream of software builders since the early ages of software development. Even as we started to build complicated user experiences, we still wanted conversational experiences.

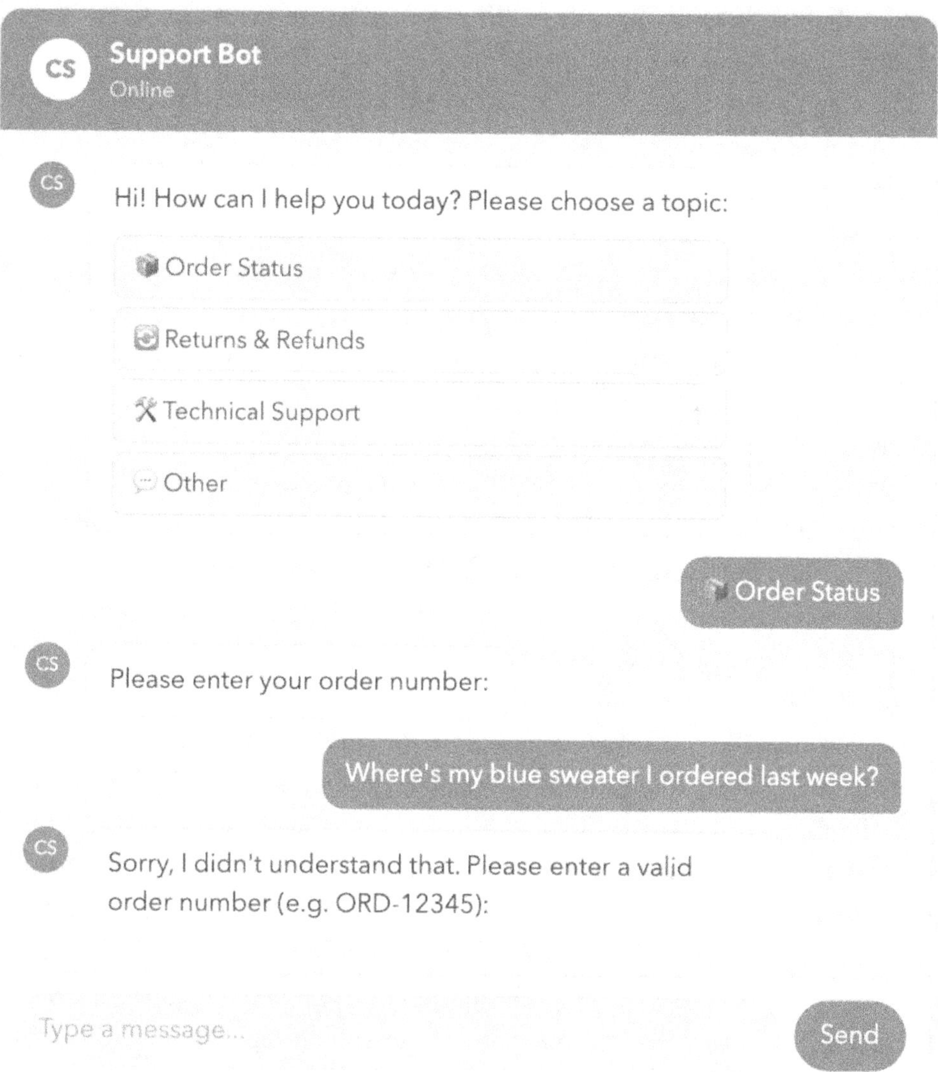

Figure 6-2. *Traditional support chatbot example. User goes off script and chatbot is unable to respond*

The problem is shown in the previous image. Before LLMs, our attempts at building conversational experiences would often result in presenting users with multiple options. The user could select an option. But they really couldn't just ask any question. The moment the user goes off script, the system fails to be useful. In the previous image, the moment the user asks a real question, the system responds with some sort of "Sorry, I didn't understand" message. Even with some extra logic, these systems never performed naturally (Figure 6-2).

For years, I think the best example of this was AGI, which I don't mean Artificial General Intelligence, I mean Adventure Game Interpreter. Sierra Online, a game company, created many games in the 1980s in which a part of the gameplay involved typing commands. These might be as simple as "open door" or "say hello." They had a basic interpreter that seemed good at guessing what you wanted. And for years, I thought this was the best example until LLMs.

LLMs provided the first human-like chat experience. The first time all of us used ChatGPT was probably a "wow, this actually works." And since then, it has only improved. The Adventure Game Interpreter was very crude in what it could understand. Changing from "open door" to "pull on the doorknob" would probably result in an error message, an "I don't understand."

LLMs overnight solved this problem! ChatGPT seemed to understand what I wanted. If those adventure games from the 1980s were made today, you could have done commands such as "pull on the doorknob," and it would have opened the door.

The solution for this in more modern games has been some sort of decision wheel. All of the game conversations unfold with the user choosing from pre-created conversation responses, pretty much like the decision trees provided by many chat systems we described before. And this has been the standard in the industry for a while. Today, because of LLMs, we can let users respond with natural text. LLMs solve the parsing problem.

Now, just because LLMs have solved, the parsing problem doesn't mean that our software systems can respond correctly. If the LLMs allow us to now understand "pull on the doorknob," we still have to have the code in place to support opening the door.

In Chapter 4, we discussed many technologies that enabled our conversations to complete actions, to do things. Without some of these enabling technologies such as RAG models or MCP servers, our conversations would be only a conversation. The ability for our conversations to take actions, or pull data enabled them to become the user interface.

Chapter 4 covers many technologies that allow us to enable our conversations, but it isn't meant to be necessarily comprehensive. And with the speed the industry is moving, new technologies and approaches will come out over time. In Chapter 4, we discussed both MCP and RAG as approaches for LLMs to access data or pull data, but there are many other models available to access data.

A common one I have personally employed lately has been a function-calling paradigm. Function calling is very similar to MCP, but it reduces the need for an extra call to another system. Function calling is often a better approach when you control both the agent and the system that the agent is calling. I bring this up here not to add more for you to know, but to make you aware that we will never have a complete list of approaches.

Think back to the support inquiry from earlier in this chapter. If we have LLMs that can understand what a user wants, but we cannot reach out to the data, we haven't made things better for a user.

But in the example below, when the user asks, "Where's my blue sweater that I ordered?" the AI Agent can go and get that data for the user. The agent can make an MCP call to our order tracking system and look up recent orders for the current user. Figure 6-3 shows and example of an AI agent responding with relevant information using context and prompt information.

These connections will allow us to create new user experiences and user interfaces that are AI-first. We will discuss AI-first in more detail later.

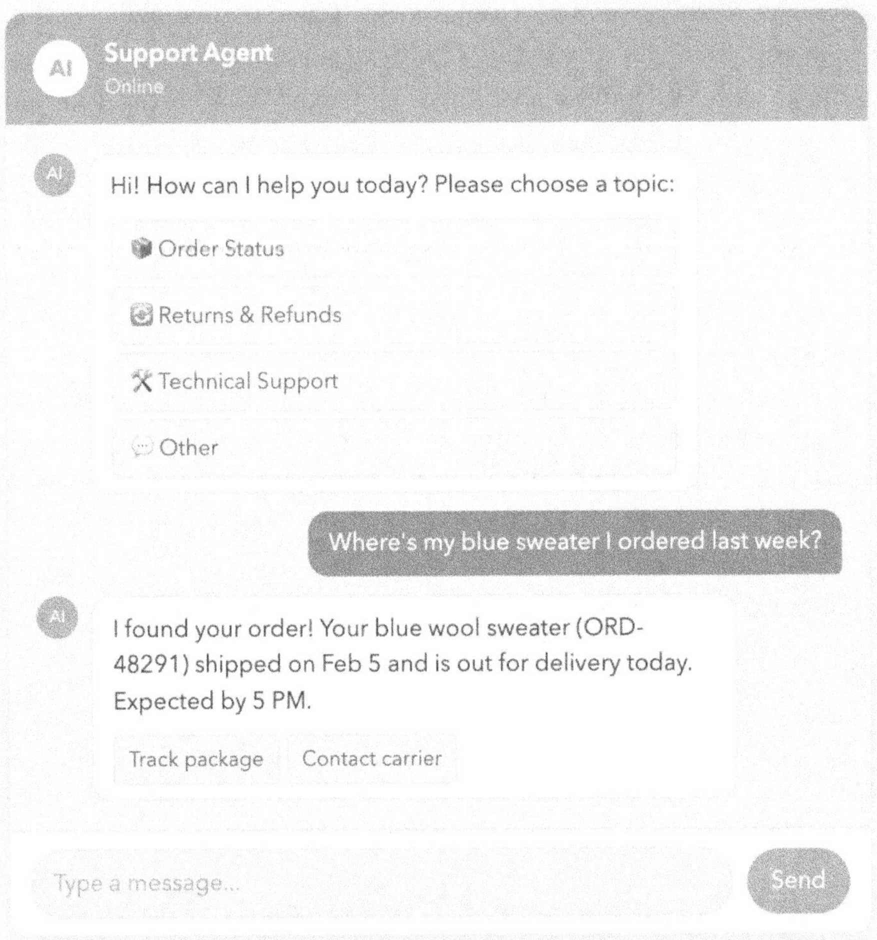

Figure 6-3. *AI-powered chatbot example. User asks a random question and AI chatbot is able to respond*

Making our systems AI-first is all about letting the AI Agent respond in the best way for the user in the current situation. Chapter 5 breaks down the challenges of introducing this concept into an existing system.

Existing systems are particularly difficult to evolve to new paradigms, both because of technical and human challenges. The human element can be challenging because we are all resistant to change. If we are to move existing users to a new way of working with our software, we must make it better than the current version. Moving users to an AI-first mode will be difficult, but if your conversations are useful to users and solve real problems, they will use them.

Multi-modal

AI-first should transcend the medium. We will first build applications that have AI at the heart, but that heart will talk to users using either web or mobile applications at first. We will build our application using AI to drive the user experience, but it will still be an HTML or mobile experience.

Once we have an AI-first paradigm in place, another option becomes available, AI agents will work better in the medium that is easier for the user. If the user wants to work in forms, the AI can generate forms for the user. If the user wants a classic chat experience, the AI will be well-suited to oblige. If the user wants to upload a picture, AI can interpret the picture. If the user wants a voice chat, AI will be able to do that, too.

Building all of this into our application would be a lot of work, but frameworks and services will be created to solve this. At the time of this writing, all the major cloud vendors have services to help create AI agents, and soon they will support this multi-modal conversation. This is a hard, but very repeatable problem. Many companies will create solutions for vendors/developers to use. There will also be a lot of open source options available. Multi-modal conversations will be so common that eventually it will become the expectation for software.

And by multi-modal, I don't just mean software supporting a voice conversation, or software supporting a text chat conversation. Conversations will be allowed to transition from chat to voice and back again. This will become an expectation for users.

Users will expect that these chat conversations are remembered between sessions. If a user is conversing with our CRM over chat, but then calls in while driving home, they will expect to continue right where they left off.

Executive Assistant

AI-first will truly change our applications when we no longer assume the AI-agent is application-specific. Many applications will become just a data source for another agent.

When thinking about creating software, we have an invalid starting point, we assume there is a user interface we must build for the user to interact with. This assumption will hold true for a lot of software, but things such as our calendar, we will probably interact with an agent on our phone going forward. Interacting with our calendar app might finally be a thing of the past (Figure 6-4).

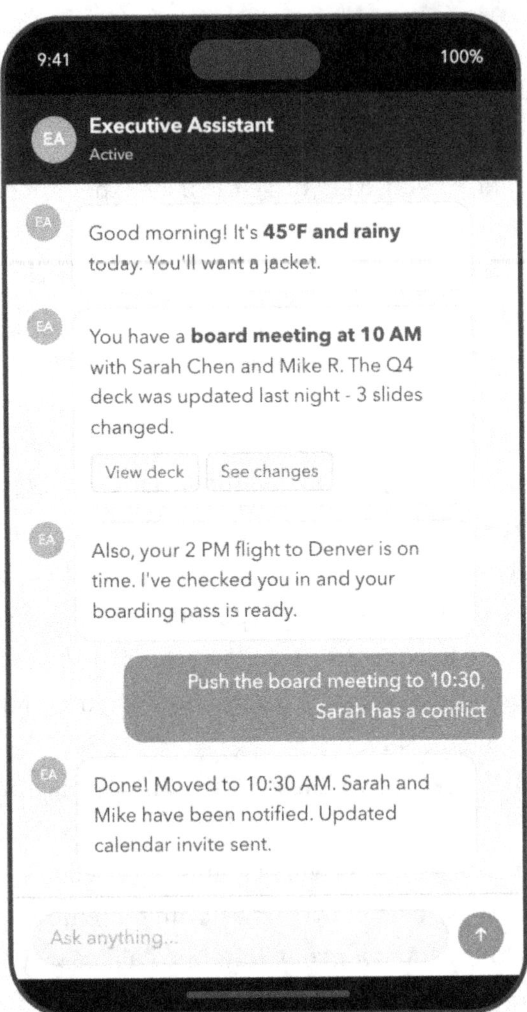

Figure 6-4. *A mobile AI executive assistant proactively provides weather, meeting briefings, and travel information while responding to scheduling requests*

Our executive assistants will have context for the calendar, but also the current weather and our travel plans. Instead of asking our phone for the weather, or using a weather application, our executive assistant will tell us when we need to know it (Figure 6-5).

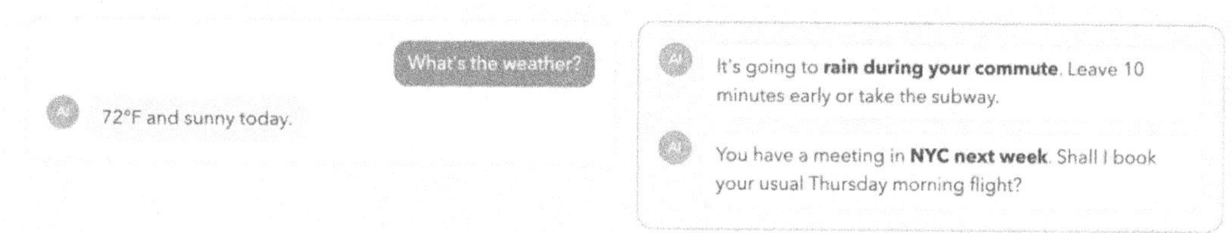

Figure 6-5. *This figure shows the comparison between asking for the current state of the weather vs. agent knowing the schedule and providing relevant weather information*

AI agents will soon be able to read the mood of our conversations. If we sound frustrated, they will be able to pick up on that frustration and respond appropriately. They will have emotional intelligence and better pick up on things like sarcasm and irony (Figure 6-6).

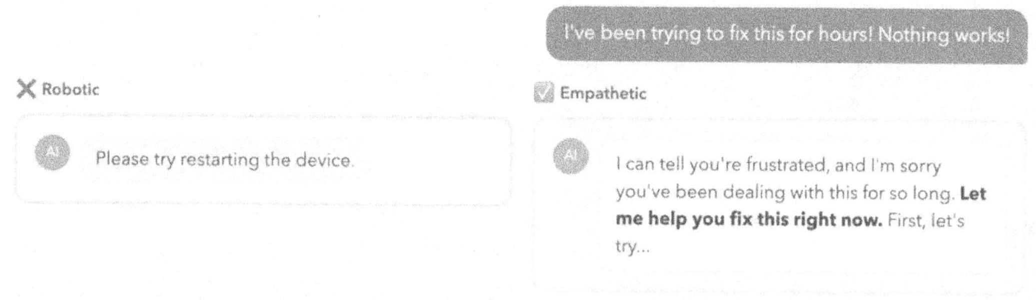

Figure 6-6. *This figure shows the comparison between a robotic response and a response that recognizes user frustrations*

Our AI assistants will learn our preferences. This sounds like a minor achievement, but often when searching for data, our preferences are critical. Imagine the scenario of searching for nearby restaurants. If my AI assistant knows I love Italian food (which is true), the assistant can do a quick look for nearby Italian restaurants instead of just generically returning all restaurants (Figure 6-7).

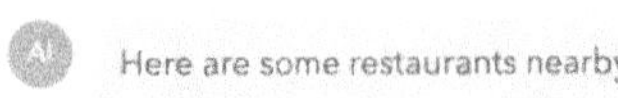

Figure 6-7. *This figure shows how an AI assistant can be personalized to recommend restaurants based on users' preferences*

AI assistants solving problems for us is going to be a difficult transition. Not because of the technical hurdles, I am confident we will easily solve those. The real challenge will be the humans. We will all feel a little uneasy about AI agents scheduling meetings for us, or telling us to take an umbrella. But we will get used to it.

AI assistants won't be without any problems. Probably the two biggest risks are security and privacy. A lot of companies will move fast to gain early market share, but many of the early movers often forget to factor in security and data privacy. When building an AI assistant, please remember that both security and privacy must be top priorities.

Specialized AI Agents

If executive assistants are coming, these personalized AI agents are basically customized to us. Every one of us has our own customized agent that will become a reality, but those won't be the only domain-specific agents.

Many domains benefit from domain-specific AI agents. Fields such as medical or legal both have very specific knowledge and a high degree of accuracy required. Wrong data or wrong responses could have big consequences. But in both cases, AI agents can provide deep help to people in those fields.

Medical (Figure 6-8):

- Diagnosis assistance

- Medical research

- Patient monitoring

Legal:

- Contract Analysis

- Research

Financial:

- Investment advice

- Fraud detection

Creative AI:

- Writing assistance

- Collaboration

- Content summarization

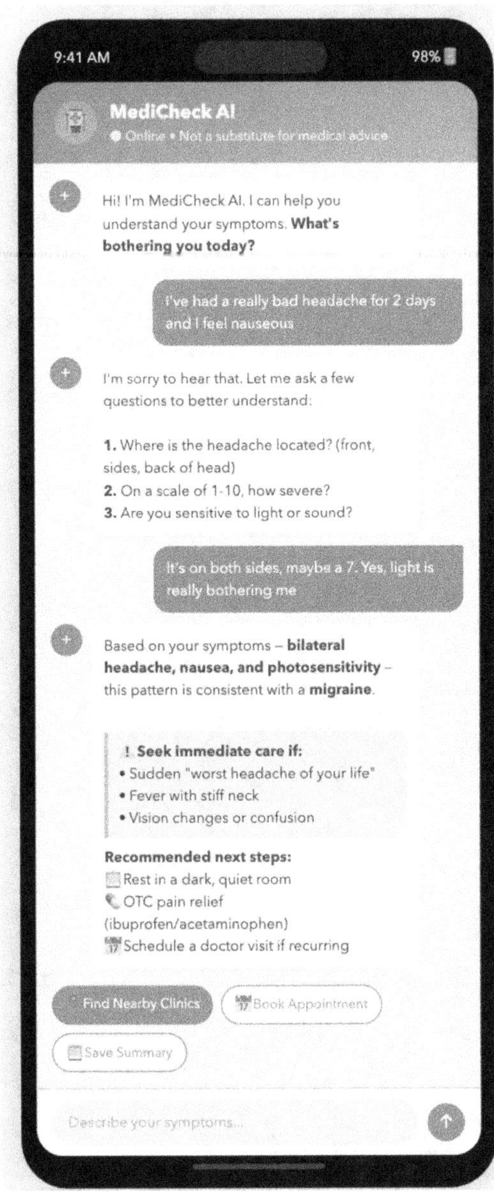

Figure 6-8. *This figure shows a medical agent conducting an assessment*

AI-First Applications

AI-first applications represent a fundamental shift in how we build applications. Unlike traditional applications that add AI as a feature to the existing application, with AI-first, the AI is the heart of the application.

AI-first applications are engineered from the ground up with artificial intelligence at their core. With these applications, AI is not a feature, AI is the core of the application.

With a traditional application, we build features that are used to achieve some goal. If we are building a traditional flight booking application, we would build numerous forms where users search for a flight. These forms would allow for filtering by price and time. Then the user would select a seat. After selecting a seat, the user might use the application to book a hotel or rent a car. With an AI-First application, the user would just state a goal, "Plan a family trip to Japan for spring break, budget $5000." The AI will figure out the available options and book the flight, hotel, and car for the user. Figure 6-9 shows a hypothetical travel booking experience with an AI agent.

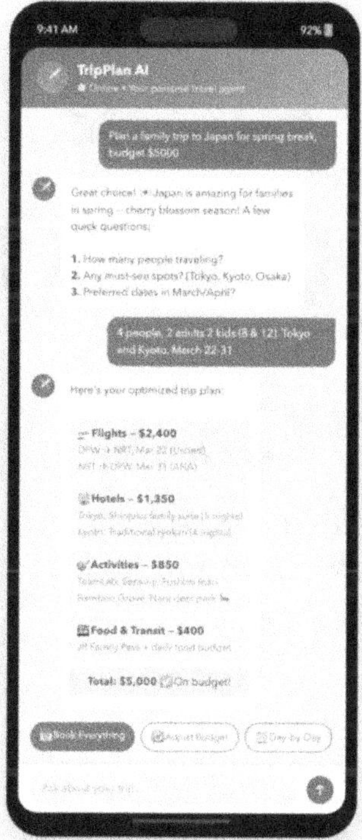

Figure 6-9. *This figure shows a travel planning application that focuses on the user's goals*

As our systems become more agentic, our agents will begin to communicate. Our agents will be communicating with other agents to solve problems for us. Instead of our software being a closed system, our agent will communicate with an agent from another system. This will allow agents to communicate with purpose-built agents.

Instead of building the entire application that does the entire trip planning, we would build a trip-planning orchestration agent. This agent would know other agents it can use to achieve the goal. The orchestration agent would use the other agents to achieve the goal as necessary. Interestingly, an orchestration agent might have to try multiple attempts to reach the goal, but the agents will be capable of doing so. Figure 6-10 shows multiple agents working together to solve a problem.

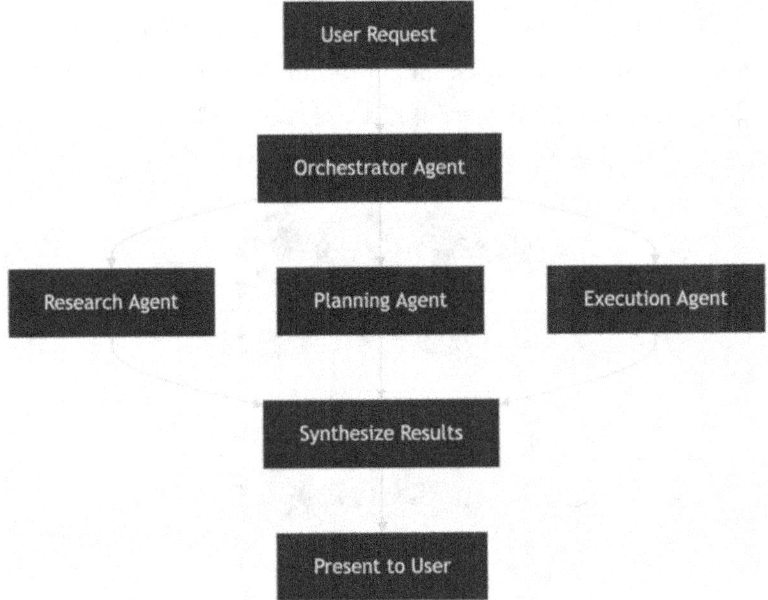

Figure 6-10. *A chart showing an orchestration agent using many other agents to achieve the goal before presenting the results to the user*

CRM AI-First

CRMs are a classic piece of software. The ability to track our sales pipelines, know the status of sales, and the desire to predict future revenue. Pretty much every organization has some sort of sales pipeline flow, and is probably tracking it in some sort of application. Almost all of those applications were built before the AI revolution.

CRMs are going to be rebuilt, with AI at their base instead of an add-on feature. Users of these new CRMs will interact through a conversation. Instead of navigating numerous forms and pages, they will just ask questions. Instead of navigating to some report, they will just ask, "Show me deals closing this month that are at risk" (Figure 6-11).

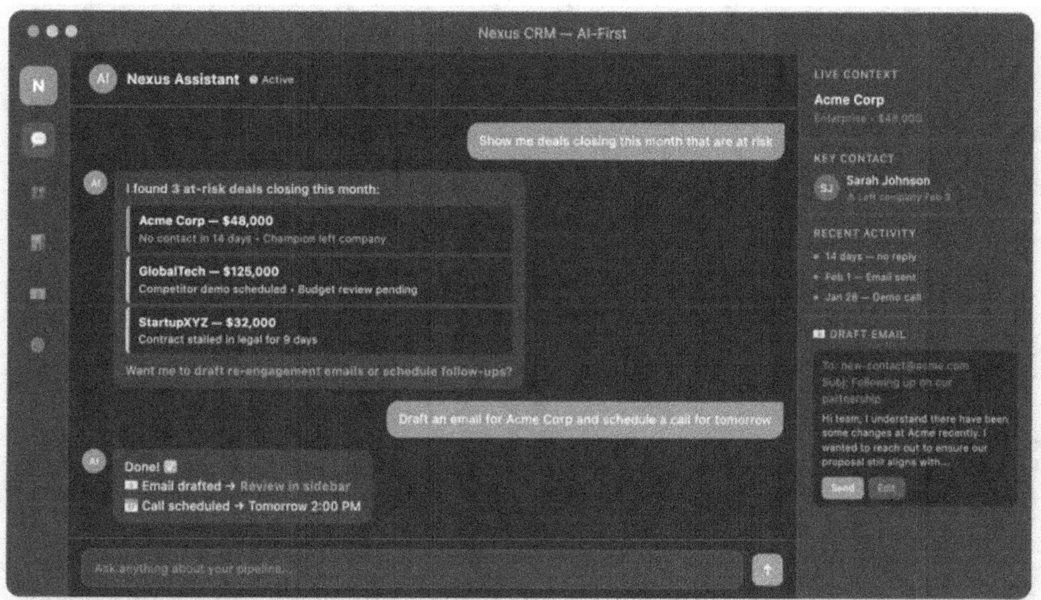

Figure 6-11. *This figure shows an AI-first CRM interface*

CRMs are interesting because they are often the center of many organizational flows. CRMs provide the source of truth for contacts, leads, deal flow, and upcoming sales for many organizations. This is living at the center, making an agentic CRM a huge value add, and an agentic CRM will need access to other systems to truly be effective (Figure 6-12).

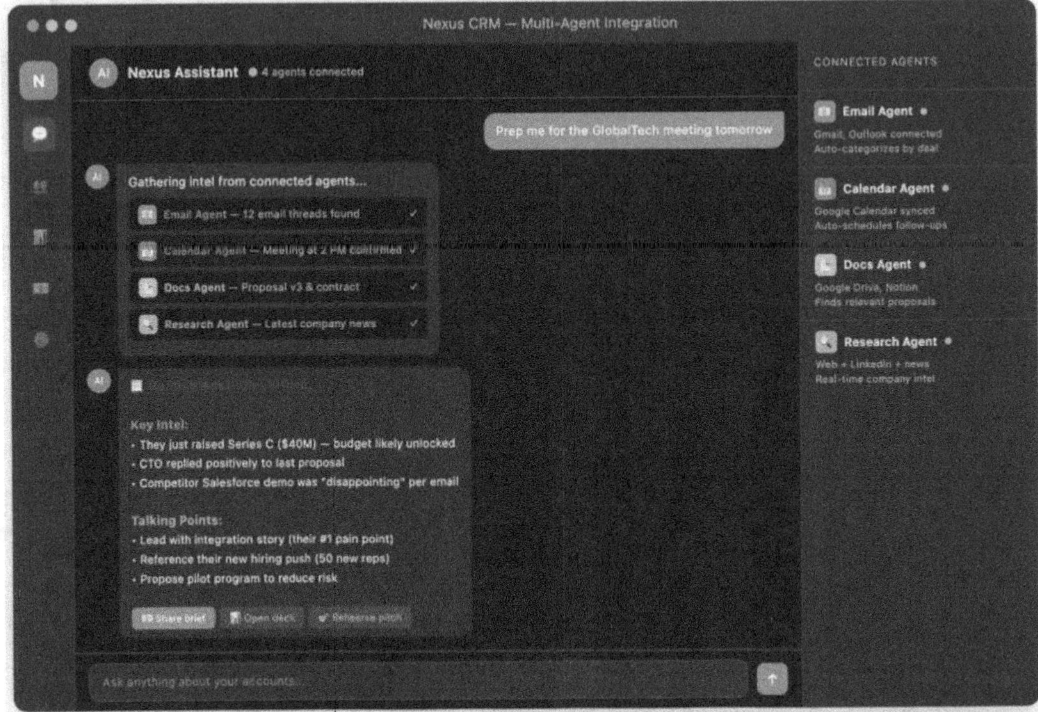

Figure 6-12. *This figure shows a CRM agent communicating with multiple other agents for things like calendar, email, documents, and research*

An Agentic CRM would not only track contacts, leads, and our workflow, but could also schedule meetings in our calendar through a calendar agent. Or email our contacts through an Email Agent. Agents communicating with other agents will change how our software works forever.

Now, a common complaint against AI-first or conversation-first experience will be, sometimes I just want a form. Our AI-first CRM could present us with a dynamically generated form if that is the best experience for this use case, see Figure 6-13.

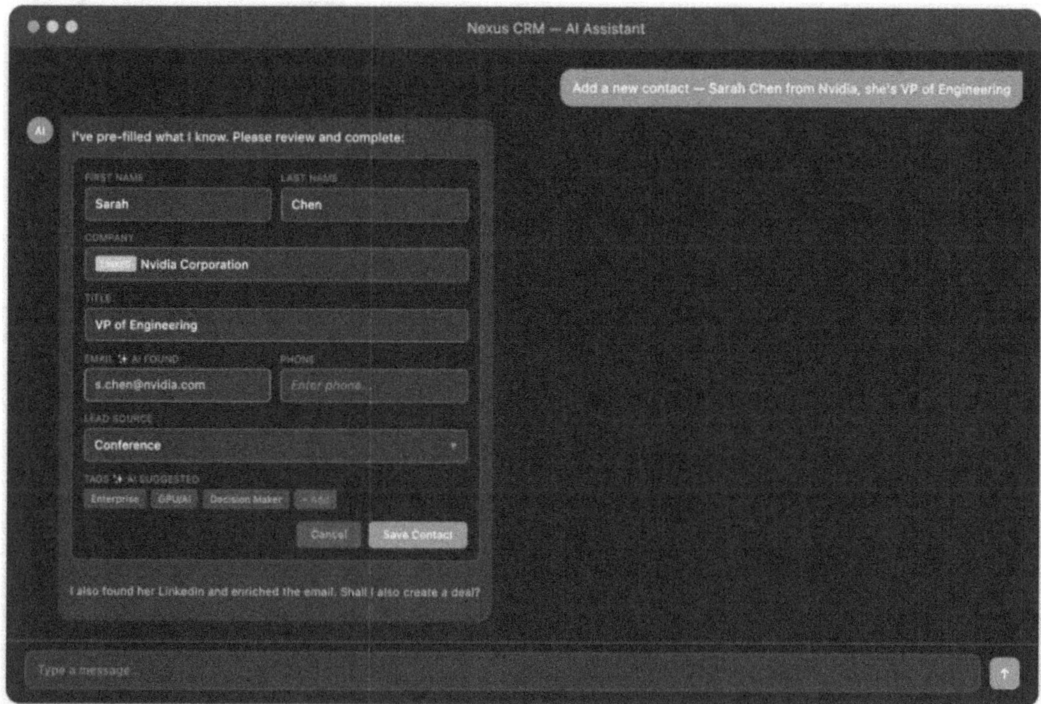

Figure 6-13. *An AI-first CRM generates a contact form when needed*

Security Concerns

Anyone reading this chapter will have a nagging feeling in the back of their head. What about the security problems this will create?

Prompt injecting is an obvious problem. With prompt injecting users inject instructions that override our system or default instructions. Users could change our scheduling agent into a document retrieval agent and retrieve documents on our behalf. Our systems can expose more information than they should, or if our systems have the ability to make changes, prompts could allow users to make malicious changes. The first solution for this problem is ensuring that agents can only operate at a certain level of privilege. If the agent is doing tasks for user "Bob," we should make sure the agent only has access to what "Bob" has access to. The next most common solution for this problem is installing guardrails around our AI agents. These effectively behave like content filters on the prompts and the outputs.

Another massive concern with moving into this AI world is sensitive data disclosure, the leaking of information to users who should not have access. Since the moment of ChatGPT's launch in 2022, this has been a well-founded concern. Again, we will want to limit the data access by user privileges, but adding an input/output filter that looks for sensitive data exposure situations, and potentially blocks conversations.

As we build these agentic systems, we should be asking ourselves two questions. Do they need access to this data to complete their tasks? If not, we shouldn't give them access. And we should also be asking ourselves, do they need to modify the data? If not, do not give them the ability to change data.

Finally, build rich logging for any agent activity. First, this can be useful for improving our agents going forward. But second, we can use this to find security problems before they are exploited.

Luddites

Any conversation on this AI revolution inevitably stirs fear of change, especially the personal question: "What will this mean for me?" A classic example of the negative impact of technology on a workforce is from early 19th-century England, with many textile workers making a good living. These workers were often doing the work their fathers did before them.

The industrial revolution changed the production of textiles; gone were the days of the artisan, and they were replaced by better processes and better tools. Ultimately, the power loom allowed for the creation of better material and faster speeds. All of this resulted in lower wages and less work for these fabric artisans.

These people were very negatively impacted. Their livelihood was changed forever. The angry displaced workers sent angry letters demanding better conditions. They signed these letters "Ned Ludd," hence the name Luddites. These letters demanded fair wages and the fair use of technology.

Their concerns and conditions were ignored. And eventually their anger grew into the destruction of machines. After the destruction and the riots, the British government responded harshly and ended the movement.

The Luddites weren't ignorant or irrational, they wanted to protect their ways of life. The technical revolution that enabled a radical change in textile production, destroyed a way of life, and the government fell on the side of the factory owners and ignored the plight of the workers.

Anytime a new technology comes along, it is easy to draw a parallel with the story of the Luddites. And this AI revolution might be the biggest innovation since the wheel. So, worries about the changes this revolution will cause are well-founded.

If you are a product designer, this will seem like a scary change. Do we need people to design software? Do we need UX/Product Designers to build mockups? I think the answer is yes. And I think talented people who can leverage these tools and patterns are more valuable than ever before. The why for this statement will be the thesis of the next section, "Loss Aversion."

Loss Aversion

Loss aversion is a cognitive bias concept introduced by Daniel Kahneman and Amos Tversky in their 1979 Prospect Theory. In short, people feel more pain for the loss than joy for potential gains.

I have often heard this described as people try to hold on to their current $100 dollars, then pursue and try to get their next $100. Losing $100 is more painful than the joy of finding a new $100.

I was first introduced to this concept in BJJ (Brazilian Jiu-Jitsu), a grappling martial art. The famed coach John Danahar talks about this in grappling. People get to a good position, but are so worried about losing the position, they don't try to advance to a better position or get a submission. They are more worried about losing what they have than moving to a better position and getting a win (submission). In grappling, I fully understand this concern. I have often gone for a submission only to find myself getting reversed and stuck in a bad position. I lost my position. These moments of loss train us to be worried about this the next time. But we must avoid this line of thinking. We must train ourselves to overcome this thinking and be comfortable with the risk.

At this point, you might be wondering, how does this apply in a book on user experience and software? Many are going to be worried about this transition to AI-First applications. Worried about job displacement, worried about changes to roles. These concerns are well-founded and real. Everyone shares them. But I think right now we need to realize we might not have a $100 to hold on to. We might not have a solid position; the world is changing that much. But that also means no one else does.

We are in an era of massive change. This can be viewed as a negative, or we can realize everyone is going through this change. We must move to these new paradigms and realize that doing nothing isn't an option. If we don't move to putting AI at the heart of our applications, we risk losing whatever ground we have.

This leads me to the point, now isn't the time to sit back and watch things change, now is the time to jump and create something new. This new world needs product designers and software architects more than ever before. Building on top of AI doesn't eliminate these roles, just changes their focus. Instead of focusing on creating the best flow of forms for a user, we will focus on ensuring our software can quickly and easily meet the goals of the users.

Sure, since the cost of building software is forever reduced, some activities are of less value than they were before. As I write this the value of writing software has most certainly been reduced by AI/LLMs that are capable of writing that software. But, making sure our software allows users to achieve their goals is at an all-time high.

We have lived in an age of mediocre software. We have talked a lot about CRMs in this book, and many big enterprise CRMs are not well-positioned to take advantage of this revolution, or at least they don't have any advantages over new players. They too need to innovate, and quickly.

This is a great opportunity for us. Since everyone is starting over, needing to rethink how our software works, now is the perfect time to invest in software. As we talked in Chapter 1, now is the time to leap into this AI-first future.

Summary

Before LLMs, conversational interfaces were rigid decision trees that didn't allow the user to stray from the script. LLMs enable software to understand free-form text, and respond in kind.

Conversations that don't achieve anything are not enough. Our conversations need to interface with our data and our systems. This is where key technologies such as RAG, MCP, and function calling come into play by allowing our conversations to read our data, or make data updates.

As we think about the future of software, software isn't a bunch of forms with the occasional chatbot, software will be primarily chats going forward. This shift to AI-first is creating a huge shockwave, but we can take advantage of this wave and create the next solutions.

Changes are scary, and all of us have a tendency to resist change. But this revolution will allow us to make better software, which is more open, more accessible, and easier to use. I understand the fear of these big changes, but don't panic, adapt.

Key Takeaways

- LLMs enable realistic conversations instead of just a decision tree.

- Other technologies, such as RAG and MCP, enable conversations to interact with our data and systems.

- Industry is ready for big changes; now is the time to act.

Index

© Chad Michel 2026
C. Michel, *From Buttons to Conversations*, https://doi.org/10.1007/979-8-8688-2688-7

Latency optimization techniques, 85
Legacy software, 9
Legacy systems, 89, 90, 93, 94
Lighthouse, 19
Loss aversion, 115–116
Luddites, 114–115

M

Medical AI agent, 106, 108
Microsoft's Clippy, 40
Mobile AI executive assistant, 104
Model Context Protocol (MCP), 78–80
Modern user interfaces
    buttons, 11
    controls, 11
    forms, 11
Modern web applications
    JavaScript-powered user
        experience, 16
    Windows Forms, 15
Monkey ladder experiment, 93–94
Multi-modal conversations, 61, 103

N

Natural Language Generation (NLG), 81
Natural Language Understanding (NLU), 81
Navigation, 32, 33
Neural network, 74
Novice, 25, 26, 49, 50, 97
Novice persona, 50
Novice's failure signals, 25

O

Orchestration agent, 110
Organizational problems, 89

P

Perceivable, Operable, Understandable,
    Robust (POUR), 18
Personalized AI agents, 106
Power user failure signals, 25
Power users, 25–27, 50, 52, 72, 97
Product designers, 16
Progressive disclosure, 23, 24, 47
Prompt injecting, 113

Q

Quick replies, 52, 56, 61

R

RAG augmentation, 78
RAG retrieval process, 77
Retrieval-Augmented Generation (RAG),
    75–78, 80
Rewrites, 88

S

Security problems, 113–114
Sierra Online, 100
Socratic method, 35
Socratic-style questions, 36
Software, 2, 3, 7, 8, 70, 103, 116
Support chatbot, 99

T

Technical challenges, 80, 89
Technical debt, 88
Terminal applications, 12
Terminal-based CRM application, 13
Text conversation, 60

GPSR Compliance
The European Union's (EU) General Product Safety Regulation (GPSR) is a set
of rules that requires consumer products to be safe and our obligations to
ensure this.

If you have any concerns about our products, you can contact us on

ProductSafety@springernature.com

In case Publisher is established outside the EU, the EU authorized
representative is:

Springer Nature Customer Service Center GmbH
Europaplatz 3
69115 Heidelberg, Germany

www.ingramcontent.com/pod-product-compliance
Lightning Source LLC
Chambersburg PA
CBHW080905160726
48000CB00009B/2866